PERGAMON INTERNATIONAL LIBRARY
of Science, Technology, Engineering and Social Studies

*The 1000-volume original paperback library in aid of education,
industrial training and the enjoyment of leisure*

Publisher: Robert Maxwell, M.C.

# Woman in the Muslim Unconscious

## THE ATHENE SERIES
An International Collection of Feminist Books
*General Editors:* Gloria Bowles and Renate Duelli Klein
*Consulting Editor:* Dale Spender

The ATHENE SERIES assumes that all those who are concerned with formulating explanations of the way the world works need to know and appreciate the significance of basic feminist principles.

The growth of feminist research has challenged almost all aspects of social organization in our culture. The ATHENE SERIES focuses on the construction of knowledge and the exclusion of women from the process—both as theorists and subjects of study—and offers innovative studies that challenge established theories and research.

**ON ATHENE** – When Metis, goddess of wisdom who presided over all knowledge was pregnant with ATHENE, she was swallowed up by Zeus who then gave birth to ATHENE from his head. The original ATHENE is thus the parthenogenetic daughter of a strong mother and as the feminist myth goes, at the "third birth" of ATHENE she stops being Zeus' obedient mouthpiece and returns to her real source: the science and wisdom of womankind.

### Volumes in the Series
MEN'S STUDIES MODIFIED
The Impact of Feminism on the Academic Disciplines
*edited by* Dale Spender

MACHINA EX DEA
Feminist Perspectives on Technology
*edited by* Joan Rothschild

WOMAN'S NATURE
Rationalizations of Inequality
*edited by* Marian Lowe and Ruth Hubbard

SCIENCE AND GENDER
A Critique of Biology and Its Theories on Women
Ruth Bleier

WOMAN IN THE MUSLIM UNCONSCIOUS
Fatna A. Sabbah

NOTICE TO READERS

May we suggest that your library places a standing/continuation order to receive all future volumes in the Athene Series immediately on publication? Your order can be cancelled at any time.

### Also of interest

WOMEN'S STUDIES INTERNATIONAL FORUM*
A Multidisciplinary Journal for the Rapid Publication of Research Communications & Review Articles in Women's Studies
*Editor:* Dale Spender

*\*Free sample copy available on request*

# Woman in the Muslim Unconscious

Fatna A. Sabbah

*translated by*
Mary Jo Lakeland

**Pergamon Press**

New York • Oxford • Toronto • Sydney • Paris • Frankfurt

Pergamon Press Offices:

**U.S.A.**                     Pergamon Press Inc., Maxwell House, Fairview Park,
                               Elmsford, New York 10523, U.S.A.

**U.K.**                       Pergamon Press Ltd., Headington Hill Hall,
                               Oxford OX3 0BW, England

**CANADA**                     Pergamon Press Canada Ltd., Suite 104, 150 Consumers Road,
                               Willowdale, Ontario M2J 1P9, Canada

**AUSTRALIA**                  Pergamon Press (Aust.) Pty. Ltd., P.O. Box 544,
                               Potts Point, NSW 2011, Australia

**FRANCE**                     Pergamon Press SARL, 24 rue des Ecoles,
                               75240 Paris, Cedex 05, France

**FEDERAL REPUBLIC**           Pergamon Press GmbH, Hammerweg 6,
**OF GERMANY**                 D-6242 Kronberg-Taunus, Federal Republic of Germany

**Library of Congress Cataloging in Publication Data**

Sabbah, Fatna A.

    Woman in the Muslim unconscious.

    Translation of: La femme dans l'inconscient musulman.
    Includes index.
    1. Women, Muslim--Sexual behavior. 2. Women,
Muslim--Conduct of life. I. Title.
HQ29.A3613   1984    297'.19783442     84-11343
ISBN 0-08-031626-3
ISBN 0-08-031625-5 (soft)

*Woman in the Muslim Unconscious* was originally published in 1982 as
*La femme dans l'inconscient musulman* by Le Sycomore, 102 Boulevard
Beaumarchais, 75011 Paris.

*Printed in the United States of America*

# Contents

# Woman in the Muslim Unconscious

Women in the Muslim Unconscious

# INTRODUCTION

# 1 The Question

Why are silence, immobility, and obedience the key criteria of female beauty in the Muslim society where I live and work? Imam Ghazzali, when he was explaining the Muslim theory of marriage in his famous work, *The Revival of the Science of Religion*, had to define the ideal woman. He described her as follows:

> On the whole, regarding the proper conduct for a wife, one can say, in brief, that she must remain in her private quarters and never neglect her spindle. She must not make frequent trips to the balcony nor spend her time gazing down from there. Let her exchange but few words with her neighbors and not go to visit them.[1]

He goes on to sketch the picture of the woman that the Muslim man must absolutely avoid as a wife — that is, the woman who represents the opposite of the ideal of desirability. One of the most serious faults that she might have, according to him, is that she might be *shaddaka*, that is, she might talk a lot.

So why are silence and immobility — the signs and manifestations of inertia — the criteria of beauty in the Muslim woman?[2] What does beauty have to do with the right to self-expression? Why, according to the canons of beauty in Islamic literature, does a woman who does not express herself excite desire in a man? Is it a fact of secondary, negligible importance, or is it a fact with a deep significance and implications that go far beyond just the sexual field and are intertwined in fields considered separate and distinct, such as the political field? Is it a secondary, superficial fact that a Muslim man's esthetic admiration and desire is for a silent woman — one deprived of power and the right to self-expression — or is this a fact that determines his choices and his political behavior at the subliminal, unconscious level? (And the more unconscious it is, the more strongly determining it is!) Is it a "purely" sexual fact that the ideal of female beauty in the Muslim cultural order specifies silence, spatial immobility (seclusion), and obedience as the qualities that are supposed to excite male desire and produce pleasure? Is this ideal unconnected with what excites the same man and produces pleasure for him in political affairs? This book attempts to throw light on these questions, not by giving an answer, but by trying to point out the elements of an answer. It undertakes to decode the messages that the Muslim cultural order has tattooed on the female body, using two discourses that have only one thing in common — the fact that they are defined as having no link to each other. These are the erotic discourse and the legal discourse. The legal discourse — that is, Islamic legality, which structures the Muslim world and its beings through its laws — is the discourse of power and legitimacy. It has a monopoly on the

3

definition and organization of reality and on the evaluation of its component elements.

According to the Islamic legal discourse, no other discourse has the right to define reality, and this is the tragedy of the Muslim progressive movements. The Left and its discourses carry no weight as long as the Islamic legal discourse asserts and claims its monopoly on the definition of reality.

The erotic discourse, on the other hand, is distinguished from the Islamic legal discourse by its not claiming to define reality, by its eminently antipower character. The erotic discourse claims to be the discourse of pleasure, and as we shall see, pleasure in the Islamic legal system is defined as an enemy of order. For legal Islam, pleasure is the generating force of subversion, and Muslim civilization is defined as an attempt to control pleasure. This book then proposes to analyze the messages which two supposedly antithetical discourses imprint on the female body: the Islamic legal discourse, the discourse of order and civilization; and the erotic discourse, the discourse of disorder and subversion.

We will attempt to discover whether the Muslim man changes focus when he passes from "the serious" (power) to the "nonserious" (pleasure), or if he remains hopelessly embedded in the same conceptual vein. Is pleasure, the erotic, an outlook different from that of power, the political outlook? Are the laws, concepts, and bases of erotic rapport different from the laws, concepts, and bases of political rapport? When a Muslim man consciously tries to detach himself from the political sphere and its laws and to turn to a woman to indulge in the delights of pleasure, does he change focus or not? (In this book, I am limiting myself to discussing solely heterosexual relationships.) Or to put it another way, what are the relationships between the political and sexual spheres in our Muslim society? It is a question that assumes great importance for me, a woman who is living, loving, working, and aspiring to happiness in a Muslim society, not only in the present, but also for the future. What are the policies that our Muslim governments — made up exclusively of persons of the male sex — might adopt in matters concerning sex? There has to be a clarification, a searching of the Muslim conscious and unconscious in order to see what is possible and what is probable and to define the limits of the impossible and the improbable.

This book is dedicated to the youth of both sexes of the Muslim countries, not because "older" people are not interested — alas, they are the ones who make the laws and govern the countries — but because the youth of Muslim countries are filled with ambition. They believe it is possible to remake the world, and they long to do so; this is their right, and it gives them their beauty and power. Through this book, which is the fruit of many long years of a mixture of pleasure and pain — and reflections on the two of them — I would like to make my contribution to going beyond the superficialities of the sexual and political discourses in which we have been submerged for almost a hundred years, ever since Kasim Amin's book, *Woman's Liberation*, appeared in the full flush of the Arab nationalist movement in the late nineteenth century.

The official statements on political and sexual matters in the Muslim societies are distressing, not simply because they are meager and lack substance, but above all because they are mechanically repeated. As an adult woman, I have heard them so much, have run into them so often in my daily search for freedom, dignity, and happiness that I feel nauseated when I hear the tedious introductory phase: "Since the seventh century, Islam has given a privileged place to woman. . . ." It is a phrase that is usually followed by an avalanche of Koranic surahs and *hadiths* that a child of eight learns in a few hours and that we adults repeat in an offhand manner throughout our whole lives without ever thinking seriously about them.

Writing this book gave me a pleasure that I discovered as a child and that I call on as an adult to defend myself against oppression and stupidity: rearranging the elements of the given adult order into another pattern that suits me better. I believe that this is a pleasure that young people indulge in more often than "older" people, not because the young are "revolutionary" by some metaphysical determinism, but simply because they have no place in the Muslim societies as they are presently structured. They find themselves with no right to work or creativity; unemployment and terrorizing oppression constitute their present and their future. It is because the young people of both sexes in the Muslim countries are not offered even the illusion of a possible "place in the sun" that they are trying to remake the world. This book is a contribution to that remodeling of the world that is our destined task and the guarantee of our survival. I would like with all due modesty to define the field and the levels of the possible and the probable in the sexual domain — a domain that this book shows to be intimately linked to, if not overwhelmed by, the political domain. I would like to say to the young men formed in our Muslim civilization that it is highly improbable that they can value liberty — by which I mean, relating to another person as an act of free will, whether it be in bed, in erotic play, or in political debates in party cells or parliament — if they are not conscious of the political import of the hatred and degradation of women in this culture. I believe human beings are capable of making and remaking their own history and that it is possible for the men and women living in Muslim societies to change the course of history, to live better, to love better. Women are not fated to live as mutilated beings.

Reflecting about what we are is a necessary step in being able to change whatever that may be. In the pages that follow we will be reflecting about how we love and what we love. As Merleau-Ponty has so well put it: "Let us try to see how a thing or a being begins to exist for us through desire or love and we shall thereby come to understand better how things and beings can exist in general."[3]

Through a number of works selected from our traditional heritage, belonging to different disciplines and cultural areas and having different aims and pretensions, we will analyze what it is that evokes the female body as an object of love and desire in the Muslim conscious and unconscious.

# 2 Framework of the Analysis

As a woman who belongs to Muslim society and has access to writing (a male privilege and the incarnation of power), I am indulging in the indescribable pleasure of rewriting the cultural heritage — a subversive and blasphemous act, par excellence. What I mean by "rewriting" is an active reading — that is, a process of decoding the heritage and at the same time of coding it in a different way. I am going to indulge myself and take the elements that have been assembled by the religious authorities and philosophers into a specific order and cut them up and reassemble them according to an order fantasized by me. And my fantasy is to try to understand how a man molded by Muslim philosophy loves a woman. Why must I be silent in order to excite the desire and win the love of my partner? Why is it that every time I assert myself, exercise my will, or attempt to escape from the control of others — in short, every time I exercise my freedom — I feel the love and desire that I inspire fade and evaporate?

Why is it that a female body and spirit that aspire to be free of control and seek to assert themselves with an autonomous will provoke anxiety and mistrust in a male partner and cool his sexual desire and love? Why does a man not desire the body of a woman who refuses to submit to his will alone? Why does a man's body burn with desire for the body of a woman that declares itself to be submissive and dominated? What are the links between desire and submission?

In order to answer these questions, I have made a selection of works from the Muslim heritage that would appear absurd to an orthodox Muslim imam, for he would find some works that he would consider sacred and others that he would consider not only secondary but utterly unimportant and insignificant. However, it is this absurdity according to the canons of Muslim orthodoxy that I claim to be the essence and the basis of my reading of that Muslim heritage. It is the distinctive feature of power to establish an order of the component elements of the world and how they should be perceived according to a given hierarchy of values in order to set up a given cultural system. I am asserting a claim to my part of that power (monopolized by men up until now in my society) by making a personal selection of works to be analyzed, which escapes the selection imposed by the religious authorities, and by giving it my personal interpretation.

The selection that I have made is composed in general of three types of works: works regarded as the foundation of Islamic legality; works belonging to erotic literature; and works belonging to what might be called the literature of chivalry — that is, treatises on love or on woman as an object of love. There is also a fourth category that is an eclectic selection ranging from treatises describing Paradise to those preparing the young Muslim man for his wedding night. These treatises are often listed by the orthodox religious authorities as being "valueless," but I regard them as having a conceptual import just as revealing as the "sacred" sources.

## THE LEGAL DISCOURSE:
## ORTHODOX, LEGAL ISLAM OR THE WORLD OF POWER

For elucidating the underpinnings of the conception of love and desire in the legal discourse, the basic documents that I will use are:

- The Koran[1]
- Imam Malik, Al-Muwatta[2]
- Imam Bukhari, Al-Sahih, with commentary by Al-Sindi[3]
- Imam Muslim, Al-Sahih[4]

As secondary sources I will use:

- Tarmidi, Al-Sunan[5]
- Imam Ghazzali, Ihya' 'ulum al-din

The legal Islamic discourse is well enough known that I need only identify it. It consists of the original legal sources, which are the Koran and the Sunna. The Koran is the book revealed to the prophet Muhammad, the Messenger of God (al-rasul); it is composed of 114 surahs (chapters), each divided into verses. There are 6,219 verses.[6] The Sunnas are "the way of acting, the behavior of the Messenger of God, shown by word (taqrir), action (fi'l), silence (sukut); they outline for the believer the way to follow."[7] The Sunnas are a source of laws like the Koran, and from this follows the importance of the correctness of the hadiths, which are statements by the Prophet's contemporaries. A hadith is:

> an account relating to a deed or decision attributed to Muhammad, an authentic documentation of some practice, whose composition has two parties to it: a chain of authorized persons certifying that the transmission of the account was made from one person to another from the last rawi [narrator] to the first transmitter. . . . "So-and-so told us, according to So-and-so, who heard it from So-and-so, who got it from So-and-so . . . so that . . . here begins the text or matn of the account."[8]

This is the reason for the importance of the date of the establishment of the hadiths. I have chosen two texts that are considered "perfect": that of Imam Bukhari (died in 870 A.D.) and that of Imam Muslim (died in 815 A.D.). Both of them are called "Al-Sahih" (The True), "because apocryphal texts have been strictly eliminated from them. Bukhari, for example, has kept only 8,000 hadiths out of more than 300,000 that came to his attention."[9]

The Sunnas of Tarmidi, on the other hand, are considered "good"; they are those that are of known origin, reported by well-known transmitters. Theoretically it is difficult to distinguish them from "perfect" *hadiths*. The question is solved in practice by the fact that the texts thus qualified have been grouped into collections and have been implemented by all jurists.

In this study I am attempting to show how representation and perception, the culture's writing about reality, become a society's definition of things and beings. In order to bring out more strongly the dimension of Islam that illustrates this point, I am going to replace the word *legal* from now on with the word *orthodox*. I will use the expression *orthodox Islam* whenever I am referring to *legal Islam*.

The *orthodox* is defined as that which "conforms to dogma, to the doctrine of a religion." The concept of orthodoxy brings out the interpretative aspect of a given heritage better than do the words *legal* or *Sunni*. The interpretative approach to a given heritage or reality is the central idea of this study, which proposes to decipher various discourses as varieties of writing, as constructions, as cultural impositions onto reality and particularly onto the female body. Contained in the idea of orthodoxy is a clear distinction between "dogma" and "interpretation." This distinction is less pronounced when one uses the adjective *legal*. So I prefer the adjective *orthodox* simply in order to bring out the interpretive aspect — here, the conventional interpretation of Islam as heritage. And every time I use the word *orthodox* it is meant to refer to legal or *Sunni* Islam. The advantage of the word *orthodox* is that it makes us aware that there are possible nonorthodox interpretations. Orthodoxy, by insisting on conformity, paradoxically contains and affirms the possibility of heresy, of different, heretical interpretations.

Orthodox Islam is being attacked every day in the Muslim countries, not only in writing, but more especially in practice. And the more decisive the attacks and violations of orthodoxy, the more urgent becomes the necessity for demanding a return to orthodoxy, to conformity to dogma as justification and absolution. As far as the female body as a political field is concerned, every new attempt to manipulate, utilize, or set up a new program for this body, more in conformity with the economic and ideological requirements of dependent societies, is expressed through a new reading of the "orthodox discourse" as the source and guarantor of legitimacy. It is this that makes this discourse interesting for us, not solely as an orthodox text fixed and established in the Sunnas, in tradition, but as the focus of interpretative strategies that one confronts every day in the Muslim world. The importance of reanalyzing orthodox Islam, and writing about the female body and sexual matters in general, is to bring to light the elements that these strategies might possibly isolate, assimilate, and copy as support for new sexual policies imposed by dependent Islamic societies.

## THE EROTIC DISCOURSE:
## EROGENOUS ISLAM OR THE WORLD OF DESIRE

The books I will be using are: *The Perfumed Garden* by Shaykh Nefzawi and *How An Old Man Can Regain His Youth Through Sexual Potency* by Ibn Kamal Pasha, who died in the year 940 of the Hegira (1573 A.D.). Although the date

of Ibn Kamal Pasha's book is very precise, that of Shaykh Nefzawi's is more
uncertain; some believe it was written in the sixteenth century, others in the
fifteenth.[10] These two books are the standard works in this field and occupy a
prestigious place in Arabic erotic literature.

Salah al-Munajid catalogued this literature of eroticism in his book, *Sexual
Life Among the Arabs*, published in Arabic in 1958.[11] The last chapter is devoted
to "Erotic Publications," which it classifies into four categories:

1. The first category is devoted to works on the arts of love and eroticism.
2. The second category is centered on the medical aspects of copulation, especially
   diet, remedies and cures for illnesses and dysfunctioning of the genital organs
   and sexual orgasm, methods of birth control, and so on.
3. The third category combines the two themes cited above, that is, erotic
   technique and the medical aspect.
4. The fourth category comprises general works which deal with themes other
   than sex, but which include mention of it. Such works include *Kitab al-
   Aghani*, by Abu al-Faraj al-Asbahani; *Al-imta' wal-munasa*, by Abu Hayyan;
   and those of Ibn Abd al-Rabbah.[12]

The two works used in this study belong to the third category, since they deal
both with technique and the medical aspect.

According to Al-Munajid, the first Arabic works of erotica appeared at the
beginning of the third century of the Hegira (about the ninth century A.D.). A
veritable explosion of those works occurred at this time, due, among other things,
to the appearance in the Muslim empire of a rich, leisured class, which consumed
pleasure and pushed the refinement of it to the extreme.[13] According to Al-
Munajid, another factor that fostered the interest of this class in eroticism was
the flood of women slaves that came to Baghdad from the four corners of the
Muslim empire: "They brought with them different and varied sexual techniques
and practices," a ploy they were supposed to have developed in order to establish
their power in the palaces of the men they were intended to satisfy.[14] The fact
that Baghdad in the time of the Abbasids was the center of power, wealth, leisure,
and erotic curiosity not only contributed to the production of an Arabic erotic
literature, but also encouraged the translation of works belonging to older civilizations, such as the Persian, Indian, and Greco-Roman. Most of the works of
erotica were written by order of the kings and emirs.[15]

The production of erotic literature reached its apogee between the ninth and
eleventh centuries; after that the writers merely reproduced earlier works or
rearranged them. The two works chosen for my analysis belong to the last century
when this literature was still being produced, although at a sharply reduced rate.
The book by Nefzawi, according to Bouhdiba, marked a veritable cutoff point,
for one has to wait until the nineteenth century before this literary genre makes
a new appearance.[16] In order to give an idea of the extent of this literature, Al-
Munajid drew up two lists of works that he himself had examined for his undertaking.
The first list was of manuscripts that had been deposited in various libraries, the

majority of which have never been published. He listed twenty-three of these.[17] The second list was of published works, and there were thirty-nine of those.

As secondary sources I have chosen two texts that are more medical treatises than anything else. They are *Al-Rahma* by Al-Suyuti and *Tashil al-manafi'* by Al-Azraq.[18]

## THE DISCOURSE OF CHIVALRY: AFFECTIVE ISLAM OR THE WORLD OF SENTIMENT

This is a series of works that treat love and desire (and woman as the object of love and desire) not only as subjects for light reading but more especially as phenomena of civilization which Muslim philosophers and thinkers had to deal with. The author who approaches love and desire as a subject for light reading is Al-Jahid in two of his famous "letters": *The Book of Women Slaves* and *The Tournament Between Women Slaves and Men Slaves.*[19] The other authors selected (religious authorities, philosophers, and thinkers) approach love and desire as very serious phenomena that confront the Muslim and for which they had to be able to find solutions within the framework of Muslim faith and law. The following books (with titles translated into English) fall into this category:

- Ibn Hazm, *The Dove's Necklace*
- Shaykh al-Sarraj, *Lovers' Perils*
- Imam Abd al-Rahman Ibn al-Jawzi, *The Disparagement of Love*
- Ibn Qayyim al-Jawzia, *The Lovers' Garden*
- Dawud al-Antaqi, *Pleasures of the Bazaar As Told in Love Stories*
- Ibn Hajla, *Anthology of Love*
- Jalal al-Din al-Suyuti, *Best Tales of Women Slaves*
- Imam Tayfur, *Women's Eloquence*
- Ibn Qayyim al-Jawzia, *Tales About Women*[20]

## THE FOURTH SERIES OF WORKS

Another series of works that I have utilized belong to other realms and fulfill other functions. Once the models, the messages, the sexual dynamics have been extracted from the legal sources of Islam, the Koran and the Sunnas, it should become possible to find their reflections in other spheres and subuniverses, especially in philosophy, the global vision of the system, the institution of marriage, and the conception of Paradise.

For gaining an overall understanding of the Muslim universe, I have chosen Ghazzali, because I have a great deal of admiration for this genius of Muslim thought, and I find enormous pleasure in observing the clarity and rigor with which his intellect moves around in the areas that he seeks to analyze.

For the institution of marriage, I have selected as a secondary source two small works that are typical of manuals for the young Muslim husband, in which the imams, charged with showing the believer the right way in all circumstances, describe to him in great detail the conduct to adopt during the first days of marriage. These manuals, like the erotic literature, form part of Muslim culture that no one speaks about but that is always available for a small price, often from street vendors who post themselves in front of the doors of the mosques or display their merchandise in the main streets of the old sections of the Muslim cities. The first one that I have used is *Qurrat al-'uyun* by Gannun al-Idrisi al-Hasani, and the second is *Adab al-zifaf* by Nasir al-Din al-Albani.[21]

For examining the conception of Paradise, I have utilized three works: the first is by Ibn Ahmad al-Qadi, the second by Al-Suyuti, and the third by Ghazzali.[22]

In the case of the erotic discourse and the legal discourse, the popularity of the works has been a very important criterion in my choice of the documents used. What we have is a selection of works that are still very widely consumed in Arab Muslim countries today. We are not talking about obscure treatises known only to an elite of experts. The popularity of these documents will allow me to advance the thesis that the models, messages, ideas, and images programmed into them are still at work in the psyche of men and women in the contemporary Muslim countries.

I have been guided in my choice by two criteria: the authenticity of the discourse and whether it remains operational in the society. Authenticity assumes a fundamental importance in this decade when the economic dependence of the Muslim countries vis-à-vis the industrialized countries (predominantly Judeo-Christian) is defined according to a time scale related to Western aggression in the area. This process began with and was embodied in the European colonization of these societies in the nineteenth century. According to this definition, what is precolonial is authentic and what is not is probably adulterated and corrupted by Western influence, which was being exerted at the time when the weakened Muslim societies did not have the power to defend themselves and to reestablish the equilibrium that normally regulates cultural relations between different societies. Most of the basic documents used in this study date from a period stretching from the seventh century to the sixteenth.

As for the concept of operationalism, it is measured on a quasi-economic scale: the consumption of the discourse. I have chosen two discourses that are still consumed by certain groups of the society in one way or another.

The orthodox Islamic discourse, given the fact that the official state machinery acts in its name, is consumed every day through the many ideological apparatuses of the state, such as the institutions of the justice system (the *shari'a*, the religious law, still regulates personal status in most Muslim societies) and of education (the Koran is taught in the schools, recited and commented on by the radio and television), to mention only the most important. As for the discourses of eroticism and chivalry, as well as the books in the fourth series, especially those I have called "manuals for the young husband" and descriptions of Paradise, the easy availability of these works in bookstores even in smaller urban centers, the great variety of editions (often pirated, the publisher rarely being named on erotic works), and the modesty of the prices (erotic works cost the equivalent of about sixty cents) allow one to assert that they are still operational and widely consumed.

All of the works used in this analysis are in the Arabic language and are regarded as an integral part of Arab Muslim culture, even though they contain very important non-Arab elements (the Persian and Hindu elements in the erotic literature are beyond question). By opting for the Arabic language, I have excluded a whole part of the Muslim world, and the field of study has been restricted solely to the Arab Muslim cultural area.

As was said at the outset, this study represents an attempt at decoding the messages inscribed on the female body by Islam as a cultural system and as a code that distributes signs and values to beings and things according to its own specific hierarchy. What this study proposes to do is decipher through the ideal of female beauty the ideological and political bases of the structuring of the libido in Arab Muslim society.

It is a question of seeing the sexual, erotic, and affective processes as the very base of the ideological process and of exposing the way in which they have been carefully separated from the political field and presented as distinct and autonomous and unlinked to the power process. [23]

In the next chapter we will examine the relationships between sex and economics and politics in dependent Islam. In the pages that follow I will try to decode the primary messages that first the erotic discourse and then the legal discourse inscribe on the female body. Then I will deal with the way in which Islam as a civilization integrates and manages first desire and then sexuality; how as a cultural system it rewrites the one and then the other. In the conclusion I will try to synthesize and identify the elements of an answer to our initial question: Does the esthetic model, the ideal of female beauty — a silent, obedient, and secluded woman — determine political models or not?

# 3 Relationship Between Sex, Politics, and Economics in Dependent Islam

In investigating the relationship between economics and sex in Muslim societies we want to identify and make intelligible the probable sexual strategies that the Muslim countries might adopt in the coming decades. This study will try to answer a precise question: How is "political power" in the dependent Muslim societies, given their cultural and economic determinants, going to exploit sexuality as a strategic area in carrying out a chosen social blueprint?

The majority of the Muslim states have officially opted for a democratic, egalitarian society. Nevertheless, there is a flagrant contradiction between what they advocate in the economic field and the decisions they make in the sexual field. While the principle of democracy and equality is proclaimed as the ideal in the economic field, it is totally rejected when sex enters the equation, and this is true no matter what the political orientation of the state may be. Two Muslim national leaders, as opposed and as different in their vision of development as the Iranian Ayatollah Khomeini and the Algerian Boumedian, are in agreement on the fact that inequality must be maintained as the organizing principle of relations in the sexual sphere.

Ayatollah Khomeini's ideal, philosophy, inspiration, and source of laws for the modern renascent Muslim society is Islam. He has required Iranian women to put on the chador again, to veil themselves. The veil has a very precise meaning: It represents the denial of the economic dimension of women, who, according to the tenets of Muslim orthodoxy, are exclusively sexual beings.[1]

Boumedian was the leader of one of the most daring movements in Muslim political life, the socialist movement. Boumedian's ideal, philosophy, and source of laws for the renascent Muslim society was socialism. Socialism, despite attempts to reconcile it with Islam, has a vision of the world essentially contradictory to the Muslim vision. Nevertheless, Boumedian took a position similar to that of Khomeini concerning the claims of Algerian women in the economic sphere. On May 8, 1966, in a speech on the occasion of International Women's Day, he revealed one of the problems that preoccupied the Algerian government: "There exists the problem of unemployment. When a job is available, should it go to a man or a woman? Should the man be left at home, while the woman is permitted to work? This is the problem!"[2]

For Boumedian, who had devoted his life to the ideals of democracy and equality, these ideals were not meant to penetrate the sexual sphere.

What are the theoretical and ideological implications of the fragmentation of the struggle for democracy into specialized areas? What is the meaning of the exclusion of the sexual area from the struggles for equality and democracy? Can

13

there be an effective struggle against the relations of inequality and exploitation in traditionally hierarchized societies with no questioning of the relations of inequality and exploitation that officially govern the sexual area?

What then are the relationships between economics and sex? Is the sexual area divorced from the struggles and transformations that people are trying to promote in the economic and political areas? Is the sexual area a miraculously neutral area?

## THE SEXUAL AREA AS A SPHERE
## OF ECONOMIC AND POLITICAL STRUGGLES

If you look only at contemporary history, you find that the sexual area, far from being neutral, mirrors with particular acuity the economic and ideological struggles of the period.

In his book, *The Surrogate Proletariat: Moslem Women and Strategies in Soviet Central Asia: 1919–1929*, Gregory Massell describes how the Russian elite, in their program of transforming the social, economic, and political structures of Central Asia, tried to manipulate the sexual area, particularly to manipulate women. The book describes not only how the Muslim women were used as the instrument for Russian aims, but also how they were used by the local populations as a means of resistance, as pawns in counter-strategies.[3]

Wilhelm Reich, in the second part of *The Sexual Revolution*, tried to elucidate another aspect of the Soviet experience, the ebb and flow that occur between sex and politics in all attempts at a radical overturn of the economic structures of society.[4]

Writing from a more general perspective, Hilda Scott tries to describe how the socialist experiment in Eastern Europe has taken over the sexual area and used the female body in its economic strategies (female labor power) and military strategies (the issue of women's right to control their fertility versus the demographic growth considered necessary for the defense of the socialist societies).[5]

Still in the socialist context, C. K. Yang in his book, *Chinese Communist Society: The Family and the Village*, describes the very tight links that connect economics and politics and sex in revolutionary strategies.[6]

There have been many studies of the multiple and inseparable connections, networks, and interactions that link the economic, political, and sexual areas in capitalist strategies. I will merely call to mind a few that are particularly relevant to our subject because they reveal how the female body is used as the field and medium of political and economic programs, policies, and aims.

In his analyses of the slave economy of the American South, Eugene Genovese shows the strategic place occupied by sex in the slave system of production and in the setting up of work and leisure relations between masters and slaves.[7] The bodies of women — those belonging to the masters as well as those belonging to the slaves — emerge in this economy as a key device in the structuring of relationships of domination and exploitation.[8]

It is always at moments of crisis that the links between economics and sex appear with the most clarity. There has been ample documentation of the manipulation of the sexual area by the fascist authorities in imposing their slogans and anxieties and in forcing individuals of both sexes to conform to the economic and political conduct that their philosophy dictated.[9] And capitalism, whether at moments of grave crisis or during relatively less disturbed periods, has always been distinguished by a particularly sophisticated interlinkage between economics and sex, especially at the level of one of the most fundamental acts of its system: consumption.[10] Michel Foucault, in the first volume of his history of sexuality, brilliantly demonstrates that the management of the sexual area is not only linked to the economic and political areas, but also constitutes the very basis of all the strategies in these two domains.[11]

But if consumption seems to be the privileged domain where economic and sexual fields intersect and are mutually supportive in industrialized countries at the economic center, this intersection assumes other shapes and takes on other characteristics in the countries along the periphery, in the dependent societies that are the subject of this study.

## SEX IN THE CONTEXT OF PERIPHERAL CAPITALISM: PROSTITUTION IN THE DEPENDENT MUSLIM COUNTRIES AS AN ECONOMIC PHENOMENON AND ITS IDEOLOGICAL EFFECTS

The imperialist expansion of capitalism in the economic field in peripheral societies is paralleled in the sexual field by some particularly striking results: first, the exploitation of female labor through the expedient of its statistical invisibility; and second, the spreading of prostitution, which is linked to the rural exodus and the exclusion of women from the education networks, occupational training, and permanent regulated jobs.[12]

The prostitution of female bodies in Third World countries — that is, their commercial consumption as sex objects — is sufficiently widespread that it affects the Muslim world as well. The same phenomenon of the linkage of prostitution with rural exodus and the economic marginalization of women shows up in Africa, Asia, and Latin America. The United Nations documents drawn up for the Copenhagen conference, whose purpose was to evaluate the progress made by the states in their policies for the improvement of the status of women, all concluded that the situation had in fact only deteriorated, especially in the countries of the Third World.[13] Claude Meillassoux, in his book *Femmes, greniers et capitaux*, explores the various mechanisms by which imperialism appropriates a labor force that is cheap only if it is especially selected out from the huge "labor pools," and he shows the strategic place of women in these manipulations.[14]

Muslim societies, despite repeated official statements of their adherence to Islam, have not escaped the decay of the institutions that once utilized women's labor — the extended family and its economic substructure, the domestic economy.

The destruction of the extended family and the collapse of the domestic economy, due to the takeover of land by the capitalist units of production, the expansion of agribusiness, and the export-orientation of the agricultural sector, have pushed the illiterate peasant women to the cities where jobs are rare, chancy, and underpaid. [15]

The expansion of prostitution among the female population, who are looking for work and poorly equipped to find it when it is available, occurs not only in the cities, but also in the rural areas and the medium-size towns that serve as funnels of immigration to the cities. The wave of prostitution assumes international proportions between the Muslim countries (for example, the expansion of prostitution in postwar Lebanon, and to Casablanca and Cairo under the influence of Saudi Arabian and Kuwaiti petrodollars), but also between these countries and Europe (especially in the case of countries that are exporters of labor to Europe). [16] A defensive silence surrounds the phenomenon of prostitution in the dependent Muslim countries. Nevertheless, since it is linked to the rural exodus and to unemployment, it can be argued that even if its rate of increase has not been proportional to these two phenomena, it has at least followed a parallel course. In the Muslim context, the deterioration of women's economic situation and the expansion of prostitution will inevitably have very serious ideological repercussions, especially on the chances for the improvement of women's status in the coming decades, and will thus become determining factors in determining specific sexual strategies.

## SEX AND IDEOLOGY IN DEPENDENT MUSLIM SOCIETIES: ABSENCE OF THE ECONOMIC DIMENSION OF WOMEN IN THE "MUSLIM CULTURAL HERITAGE"

Two fundamental facts are likely to determine the sexual strategies of Muslim societies in the coming decades.

The first is their economic dependence, which makes the bourgeoisie of these countries unable to provide jobs for a population with one of the world's highest birthrates. The importing of sophisticated technology from the industrialized countries, the exporting of barely processed raw materials, and the export-orientation of the agricultural sector are all factors that inhibit the creation of jobs and exacerbate unemployment. Moreover, unemployment means a decline in men's purchasing power and in patriarchal authority, and thus brings about the collapse of the family as an institution that provides for the needs of women and children. The result is the emergence of millions of women and children as job seekers on the national employment market.

The second fact is that Muslim culture has a built-in ideological blindness to the economic dimension of women, who are ordinarily perceived, conceived, and defined as exclusively sexual objects. [17] The female body has traditionally been the object of an enormous erotic investment, which has clouded (if not totally hidden) woman's economic dimension. In addition, the inflation of the erotic dimension of women has resulted in the eroticization of the male body, the general eroticization of relations between the sexes, and thus an exaggerated preoccupation with sex and the sexualization of problems belonging to other spheres of life. For example, given the exaggeration of the erotic dimension, certain economic problems are experienced as sexual problems. This is the case with a man's economic failure. The unequal distribution of wealth, widespread unemployment, and the chancy character of jobs and wages reduces the buying power of males (if they have any). And since virility in patriarchal Muslim society is defined in terms of economic power, economic failure is experienced by the male as castration, as a problem with virility, as impotence.[18]

In the same way, the invasion by women of economic spaces such as factories and offices, which is an economic fact of development, is often experienced as erotic aggression in the Muslim context, where the female body, defined as 'urya (nudity), has been neutralized by the traditional structuring of space (seclusion of women and the wearing of the veil when moving through male space).

## THE FEMALE BODY AS MEDIA:
## DECODING MUSLIM PATRIARCHAL WRITING
## THROUGH THE EROTIC AND LEGAL DISCOURSES

One of the contributions of the social sciences, particularly anthropology, psychology, and sociology, has been to show how the human body is used to support power struggles, as a place where the dominant group inscribes its systems of domination, its taboos, and its punishments. But if this is true for the human body in general, it is all the more true for the female body, which seems to be the prime material for the symbolism of power and writing on hierarchy, domination, and exploitation. The female body as a field of writing, initiation, and discourse on power, domination, and exploitation seems to be a constant aspect of human societies, whatever the degree of development of their means of production.[19]

In the pages that follow I propose to decode the messages programmed onto the female body by centuries of Muslim culture, using two discourses that form part of the heritage defined as authentic and not influenced by the West and its conquests. This decoding is a necessary preliminary exercise for identifying some elements of the answers to the following question: What sexual strategies are Muslim societies likely to adopt, given their economic and ideological determinants?

The difficulty that Muslim societies, including their politicians and scholars, have in perceiving the economic dimension of the female person in the twentieth century is all the more significant in that the economic discourse is a dominant one. The twentieth century is a period when nation-states, whatever their level of development, use statistical methods that play a decisive role in the evaluation of the contribution of each individual to the creation of national wealth. It is obvious that these methods and the theories about them, above and beyond their avowed aim of quantifying production and the distribution of wealth, function as ideological devices for legitimation, hierarchization, and manipulation. The fact is that these statistical methods have a problem in quantifying the productive potential and economic contribution of the Muslim woman.

This gives rise to our interest in discovering how power has coded female potentialities in our cultural heritage. And the orthodox discourse is precisely the discourse of power — rather, it is power.

One might ask what interest there can be in comparing two discourses so different as the erotic discourse and the orthodox discourse. The interest lies precisely in the relationship that the two discourses have to power. The erotic discourse is a reflection by a human being — the author — on a precise subject, which is specifically the female body, regarded as a source and instrument of pleasure.

The orthodox discourse, on the other hand, is the discourse of a god on power and its dispensation; it is the source and origin of a vision that takes total charge of the organization and management of the universe and everything in it, including pleasure. The orthodox discourse is power, the exercise of power, and the delegation of power, all in one.

The nature and scope of the two discourses and their resulting impact on the Muslim psyche are entirely different in kind. The erotic discourse is an individual reflection, the personal opinion and beliefs of Mr. X or Mr. Y on the female body as the seat and agent of sexual pleasure. The motivation of the authors is to throw light on an important but murky and inexplicit aspect of the life of the Muslim community—sexual desire. It is not their intention to impose on readers their own vision of the female body and its purpose. Moreover, they take all the methodological precautions necessary to maintain the uncertainty that characterizes their approach. They rely on Allah to put them onto the right track, because the believers are the audience for their books. The authors' relationship to power is totally negative; they do not claim to possess the truth nor to dispense it. What they claim to do is share information on a very mysterious subject—the female body as a source of pleasure.

The orthodox discourse, on the other hand, speaks in a completely different voice — one of power. It is not the work of a person; it is a work of divine inspiration, which imposes itself as the collective, global, total, and totalitarian vision of the universe. With the erotic discourse one is in the realm of individual reflection, of the profane — in short, of the human. With the orthodox discourse, one moves to the diametrically opposed realm of the sacred, which is in essence collective and divine.

The effect of these two discourses is totally opposite. The erotic discourse is an optional discourse, with each believer able to decide for himself or herself to read or not to read this literature. The orthodox discourse is a compulsory, omnipresent, omniscient discourse. One cannot escape it as a member of the

Muslim community; it is time and space, it is the air that one breathes, the relationships that one has, the food that one eats—it is life itself. The orthodox discourse is diffused into the flesh and nerves of a person from the first moments of existence, and even before, because at the moment of copulation the believer utters a ritual prayer. At birth a whole series of prayers and invocations combined with an animal sacrifice create a social niche for the newborn. The latter will be bathed throughout childhood in the orthodox discourse, which constitutes the matter and method of Koranic teaching. Circumcision, as a rite of passage and admission to the status of conscious being, tattoos the collective prohibitions onto the body of the male child through a bath of blood.

The consciousness of the circumcised child is the consciousness of having become a member of the Muslim community, which fetes him and takes charge of him. Beginning at that moment, the life task of the young adolescent is to learn how to live up to the expectations of the orthodox discourse, how to be a good Muslim. The orthodox discourse is the determining influence on the Muslim individual's personality, which it shapes, molds, and directs at the preconscious level as much as at the conscious level. It is this that lends importance to the analysis of this discourse as it relates to the totality of life — to the natural as well as the human environment.

# PART I
# THE RELIGIOUS EROTIC DISCOURSE:
# THE FEMALE BODY AS THE PRODUCT
# OF MALE PLEASURE

# 4 Genesis of the Erotic Discourse

The Muslim erotic discourse grew out of the desire of the guardians of religious conduct, the theologians and legal experts, to answer the question that at some time or other the Muslim believer is led to ask: How should one make love when one is a Muslim? What are the rules that regulate what is permitted and what is forbidden in the act of copulation? The erotic discourse is religious because it is an attempt by the sheikhs, imams, and qadis — the religious authorities vested with the responsibility for guiding and channeling the acts of the believer — to clarify for him the conduct to adopt toward one of the most mysterious areas of creation: sexual desire. It is a very rich literature.[1]

I have concentrated my analysis on two works that are particularly popular, because they are available for a pittance in the streets and bookshops of the old sections of the Muslim cities. They are: the book of Shaykh Sidi Muhammad Nefzawi, entitled *The Perfumed Garden*,[2] which sells for the equivalent of forty cents; and *How An Old Man Can Regain His Youth Through Sexual Potency*, which costs about sixty cents and is the work of the "savant of the century, unique in his time, the honorable Mawla Ahmad Ibn Sulayman, famous under the name of Ibn Kamal Pasha, who died in the year 940 of the Hegira."[3] The first book was written in the twelfth century, and the second in the fifteenth.[4]

The aim of this literature was essentially religious. The purpose of the authors was to serve the *umma*, the Muslim community. The first book (*The Perfumed Garden*) resulted from an order. What happened was that a vizir, after having become aware of a first version of the work, commissioned the author to rewrite it. The vizir commented to a blushing and disconcerted Nefzawi, whom his emissaries had found in southern Tunisia: "You are not the first who has treated of this matter. . . . I swear by God that it is necessary to know this book. It is only the shameless bore and the enemy of all science who will not read it."[5] And it was as one of the faithful, called upon to carry out a privileged task, that Nefzawi asked for God's help in beginning his work:

> I forthwith went to work with the composition of this book, imploring the assistance of God (may he pour his blessings on his prophet, and may happiness and pity be with him).
>
> I have called this work *The Perfumed Garden for the Soul's Recreation*.
>
> And we pray to God, who directs everything for the best . . . to lend us His help, and lead us in good ways.[6]

The second author, Mawla Ahmad Ibn Sulayman, who wrote his book thanks to the encouragement of Sultan Salim Khan, had a natalist objective:

I have written this book, but my aim in doing it is certainly not to play a part in inciting debauchery or encouraging sin; my aim is not to help the voluptuary who violates the commandments and makes licit what Allah has declared to be illicit. My aim is to come to the aid of him whose desire does not result in the achievement of that which is permitted and which is the source of populating the earth and increasing the race — an idea which expresses the counsel of the Prophet (may peace and prayer be with his soul): Copulate and reproduce yourself, so that I may be proud of you before other nations.[7]

While the first writer asked God to help him contribute to the scientific knowledge of the believer on the subject of copulation, the second stated his wish to help the believer to be fulfilled within "what is permitted" and thus contribute to the multiplication of the members of the *umma* and carry out the natalist wish of the Prophet. Both works include a detailed table of contents to facilitate their use and to increase the benefit that the believer could draw from them. It goes without saying that the two documents are addressed to a male reader, despite the fact that the obsessive subject of the two works is woman, her body, desires, wantonness, and mysteries.

This woman is depicted as an omnisexual woman, a creature whose most prominent attribute, which determines her whole personality and behavior, is her sexual organs, called in Arabic *al-farj*, whose "proper meaning," according to Nefzawi, is "slit, opening, passage; people say 'I have found a [*farja*] in the mountains' "[8] — that is, a crevice, a crack.

From the fact that this woman is described through the characteristics of this crack, which is not only an autonomous force but also a determining force for the whole female personality (Chapter 5), arises the question of how she can be satisfied. What kind of copulation does she require? How does she reach orgasm and under what conditions (Chapter 6)? From the answers to these questions emerges the outline of the man who has the power to satisfy this woman-crack. It is a man fashioned in the image of the one whom he is intended to satisfy, to fulfill, to serve. Like her, he is omnisexual, defined and determined by a phallus-shaft, corresponding to the vagina-crack (Chapter 7).

# 5 The Omnisexual Woman: A Voracious Crack

The omnisexual woman is woman-as-body, exclusively physical. Her other dimensions, especially the psychological, economic, and engendering dimensions, are not reduced or marginalized; they are nonexistent. Their absence is symbolized by two attributes much prized in this woman-as-matter — silence and immobility: "She speaks and laughs rarely, and never without a reason. She never leaves the house. . . . [and] gives her confidence to nobody."[1]

The omnisexual woman who emerges from the erotic discourse has the lack of consciousness of the female archetype described by Erich Neumann and the inertia of the Earth Mother found by Bachofen in his excursion into the mists of prehistory.[2] The eclipsing of the psychic dimension of this creature, the annihilation of the ego are carried out by the simple omnipresence of the physical dimension. The omnisexual woman is a woman of never failing patience, of ample, engulfing flesh, supported by thighs hard as pillars. Her physical attributes (shoulders, arms, forearms, mouth, lips, cheeks, face, eyebrows, forehead, hair, neck, breast, waist, belly, hands, feet) are minutely captured in a rigid robot-like portrait in which whiteness of skin and blackness of hair take the lead. But the most important element in this portrait, which determines the character of the woman and thus the universe that is structured around her desires, is what she has between her legs:

> The lower part of the belly is to be large, the vulva projecting and fleshy, from the point where the hair grows, to the buttocks; the conduit must be narrow and not moist, soft to the touch, and emitting a strong heat and no bad smell; she must have the thighs and buttocks hard, the hips large and full.[3]

Moreover, certain physical attributes, easily seen because exposed to view, like the mouth, lips, breasts, tongue, nose, ears, color of eyes, chin, neck, provide precise information about the emotional capacity of this woman and the shape of the vagina, especially its narrowness. The three elements — physical attributes, shape of the sexual organs, and emotional potential of the woman — form a triangular mirror-game. Each of these elements reflects the other two, is reflected in them, and the total effect of these reflections constitutes and incarnates the omnisexual woman. The characteristics of the visible features reflect the size, volume, and color of the omnipresent genital organs. A small red mouth and hard, full breasts indicate a narrow, hot vagina, inexhaustible resources of tenderness, and high intelligence. A large mouth reveals an enormous vagina, and vice versa. A red or short tongue is an infallible sign of a damp and

25

cold vagina. Large nostrils indicate an insatiable vagina. A small chin suggests that the vagina is as narrow as a man could desire. A fat woman with a thick neck is to be avoided; she hides between her legs an enormous vagina difficult to fill. In the omnisexual vision, exterior characteristics become mere props, reflections, and signs of the central element, the crack, the slit, the woman's sexual organs, which ideally should have three characteristics to produce happiness for the believer — narrowness, heat, and dryness.[4]

But in this vision, the woman's sexual organs — far from being moved by any desire to please the believer or Him who created him, Allah, the Almighty — constitute an autonomous, formidable force, insensitive to all morality and unaffected by any idea of limitation, order, or hierarchy. The erotic discourse, elaborated to satisfy the curiosity of Allah's representatives on earth, the viziers and kings, structures for an audience of believers an omnisexual woman who has arisen from the deepest layer of the unconscious. She emerges from all that has been forgotten, rejected, repressed, forbidden; from the premonotheistic, pre-Islamic period, the era of barbarism, *al-jahiliya*, the era of no limits, of no thresholds, the era of the goddesses, when the identity of a child was determined by its maternal origin, the vagina from which it emerged, and not by a fiction, a law — that is, paternity.[5]

The erotic discourse lays out for the imagination of the believer the mirage of a not distant past of the Muslim East, when women fostered creation on earth and in a serenely female heaven. The birth of the male God, Allah, took place in an iconoclastic fury in the temple of the Kaaba in Mecca, where the idols that put up the strongest resistance to destruction were those of the goddesses Al-Lat, Al-Uzza, and Manat.[6]

In the erotic discourse, woman's sex is viewed by the men who approach it as a pole of animal energy, irresistible, vibrating, and making the universe vibrate to a rhythm all its own, where the male body is reduced to simply looking on, hypnotized: "[She] laid herself down upon her back, baring her thighs. . . . Then I examined her vulva. . . . It opened like that of a mare on the approach of a stallion."[7] The omnisexual woman moves in zones where distinctions between animal and human no longer exist. The female sex is elsewhere described in the following terms: "When [it] is provided with ample flesh, it resembles the head of a lion. It is called *vulva*. Oh! how many men's deaths lie at her door?"[8]

It is thus not surprising that when this sex is agitated by the desire for copulation, the body that it inhabits can only follow its impulses: "When the body of my visitor was fixed on copulation, a wild desire was aroused between her legs and her private parts were seized by convulsions."[9]

It is no wonder that this sex, an energy pole, a seat of agitations and convulsions, sends out its rays like radar in search of the phallus. It takes on various aspects and rhythms, and each type is described and given a name. There are voracious sexes able to seek out and draw the available prey from within the surrounding space:

[The yearning one] is burning for a member, and, having got one in its embrace, it refuses to part with it until its fire is completely quenched.

Certain vulvas, wild with desire and lust . . . throw themselves upon the approaching member . . . as if in fear that, unaided, it could not find the [matrix].[10]

This voracious sex is programmed for the orgasm that it knows how to pursue obsessively by muscular reflexes and pure biological vibrations, which reign supreme in this universe:

When this vagina [the restless] has received the member it begins to move violently and without interruption until the member touches the matrix, and then knows no repose till it has hastened on the enjoyment and finished its work.

[The assistant] is thus named because it assists the member to go in and out, to go up and down, in short, in all its movements, in such a way that if it desires to do a thing, to enter or to retire, to move about, etc., the vulva hastens to give it all facilities, and answers to its appeal. By this aid the ejaculation is facilitated, and the enjoyment heightened.[11]

The vagina is thus equipped to seek out, ingest, and manipulate the instruments capable of giving it orgasm. In the wake of that, the authors ask the question so central to those who live in a social order where woman's sexuality is supposed to submit to a multitude of detailed constraining regulations and restrictions: What are the limits of this voracious vagina? To what lengths will it go as it plays out its desire? Will it reach a point where it will be sated, or is it insatiable in its search for instruments of pleasure? Who but women could answer these questions? The women's responses were unanimous, and moreover men approved them. There was a consensus that woman's desire surpassed by far that of man:

Some people have said that the sexual appetite of woman is greater than that of man. Others have said that while woman is never sated nor exhausted by copulation, man, on the contrary, is very quickly sated and exhausted, and his desire to copulate ebbs if he indulges in it immoderately. If one copulates, it seems, night and day, for years and years with a woman, she never reaches the point of saturation. Her thirst for copulation is never assuaged.[12]

There is the case of a king who had 360 concubines, each of whom, according to the rotation that is required in a polygynous situation, had the right to be honored by his majesty one night per year. This is supposing that his majesty, despite the energy required for the daily duties of royal power, had the strength to copulate daily with unfailing regularity with all the women he had succeeded in making his own. The author does not inform us on this point, but it is implicitly assumed in the text that the virility of the king was great enough to bring joy once a year to each of his concubines. One feast day when his majesty was feeling especially euphoric and well disposed toward the women of his harem, he asked them to dance and sing for him. Wine flowed, and he rashly promised to grant the wish of each of his concubines, if she expressed it. One of them expressed the wish to copulate to the point of satiety. The king was furious and ordered a thousand men to sleep with her that night, but she was far from being satiated. Then the king called together his counsellors and asked their help in solving this enigma. They advised him to kill her because she "threatened to debauch the whole population of the town,"[13] and the wise men gave him the following assessment:

> Woman only appreciates life if one copulates with her, because her body grows and develops, she blooms and is rejuvenated when she smells the scent of a man. Copulation brings her great pleasure and tremendous joy, especially when the copulation is varied. For woman each variation has a particular nuance, and she rates each improvisation according to the partner who unstintingly enacts it for her.[14]

Coitus has an opposite effect on each of the sexes. It energizes one of them and weakens the other. It makes woman bloom and man wilt.[15] It is not surprising that the next step in this system of reasoning is the assertion that the only males equipped to cope with this voracious-crack woman are not men, but animals, and it is especially the ass that plays the starring role in the universe of the erotic discourse. The ass has the ideal instrument to satisfy the female sex, and (as we shall soon see) it is the standard against which men's performance, in terms of the size of the penis, is measured and its potential evaluated. There is a whole series of male fantasies that revolve around the idea of copulation between woman and ass.

In one of these fantasies, the coupling is discovered by a porter who earns his living by hiring out an ass to those who need it for hauling loads. His attention is attracted by a beautiful young woman who comes every day to hire the animal and only brings it back very late in the afternoon. The ass is always fresh and fit after what is supposed to have been a hard day's work, and it is this that puzzles him. So he decides to follow the woman to find out where she takes the beast. It is an ill-fated day. From his hiding place by the front door through which the unknown woman had disappeared with the ass, he hears the screams of an old woman. The animal had just ripped open his partner, who had lost control and had not pricked the penis of her fiery companion soon enough. That day her pleasure had been so intense that she had forgotten to use her needle to control the ass's penis, and in its excitement it had plunged in its organ and ripped open her belly in full orgasm. The old lady (always an evil figure in the omnisexual universe) describes to the curious porter the exploits of the couple whom she regularly assisted, and does so with the wealth of realistic detail that is the staple of fantasy:

"I brought up this child, who is the daughter of a great merchant. Her parents died in this very place, and she was left alone. She had inherited money and gold and continued to live here. One day she came with that ass, and she trained it so that it would mount her two or three times a day, between the time that she took it from your place and the time that she returned it to you. She laid in stocks of carefully selected barley, grain, and cold water, and she was constantly feeding it." "And how did the ass manage to mount her?" asked the porter. "I will show you," whispered the old woman. "She led me," related the porter, "to a part of the courtyard where the young woman had built a hillock on which she would stretch out in order to let the ass mount her, and so she could easily wrap her legs around it." "Why, then," he asked the old woman, "if she could accept the ass so well, was she killed this time? Why did the ass rip her open this time?" "She used to use a needle," explained the old woman, "that she held in her hand to control the length of the penis that she wanted inserted into her vagina. When the ass got all excited and wanted to push further in, she curbed its ardor by sticking the needle in its penis at the point which would achieve her aim. But this time she seems to have lost control of the situation. At the moment of orgasm she must have forgotten to stick the needle in at the usual point, and the ass ripped her open by thrusting its whole penis in." The porter related that he examined the hand of the dead young woman, and that he really did find a needle between her clenched fingers, which corroborated the old woman's account. "I asked her," continued the porter, "how she managed to get the ass to copulate with her the first time." The old woman responded that the first time the young woman brought a she-ass, which she let the ass approach; when it was excited to the point of protruding its member and wanted to mount the she-ass, the young woman pushed the she-ass aside, lay down in its place, took the member of the ass and introduced it into her own vagina, and the ass carried on.[16]

To the great surprise of the porter, the old woman concluded by telling him that many important men, rich merchants and great notables, had asked for her hand in marriage, and that she had declined all offers by claiming that she had forbidden herself all contact with men.

There is the story of another woman, much more brazen than the first one, probably because she was less bourgeois, who arranged to have her ass at home right under the nose of her husband, who never suspected his wife's tastes, even after having caught her *flagrante delicto*:

The tale is told of a man who was a porter and owned an ass which he used for carrying his loads. He had a passionate wife who loved sexual union and couldn't go a single day without it. Her vagina was so deep that only a shaggy object of huge size was able to please her. Her husband copulated with her very infrequently. When he came home after work, he seemed exhausted and worn out; he ate dinner and then went to bed, leaving his wife the job of watering and feeding the ass. The woman then went to where the ass was, placed the animal's packsaddle on her own back, took some of its dung and urine in her hands, mixed it with water, and smeared it on her private parts; then she got down on her hands and knees in front of the animal. The animal approached her and smelled her. Believing that it was a she-ass in front of it, it protruded its member and jumped on her. The woman took its member in her hand, rubbed it between the lips of her private parts, and let it glide into her until it disappeared. Then she squirmed with the member of the ass inside her, until her orgasm came. The ass became used to these operations, which pleased it. Every time that the woman came near, it protruded its member.[17]

One night when her husband wanted to copulate with her and couldn't find her, he went looking for her and found her beneath the beast. She explained to him that she was making an experiment by trying out the ass's load in order to have an idea of how tired it got every day. She said that she went so far as to put the load on her back in order to take better care of the ass. According to Nefzawi, who included this story in his chapter entitled "On the Deceits and Treacheries of Women," the husband never suspected anything.

But these women can't compete with a slave belonging to a black king, who was able to take on an ass as dessert after having copulated with an army of 300 men. The story leads one to believe that she was black skinned. (The importance of this detail in the Arab Muslim imagination is well known, especially as it surfaces at the level of the fantastic in the *Arabian Nights*.)

It is told that the king of the blacks had sent his army to fight one of his enemies. When they defeated the enemy, they managed to capture one of his concubines whom he had banished from his bed and who was in disgrace. When they saw her great beauty and grace, the soldiers told each other that she was fit for no one but their king. "I am not fit for him," she said. "Why not?" they asked her. "My master," she responded, "ordered his slaves — and there were 300 of them — to copulate with me, which they did, but my desire to copulate was far from being assuaged, still less from being sated. He then ordered me sent out of the town. I asked the man charged with carrying out the order to take me far away from the town. When I arrived in the countryside, I saw an ass mounting a she-ass, and its penis was in full erection. When I saw it, I couldn't control myself. I bought the she-ass, and I placed myself under its companion. It jumped on me with a sex whose parallel I have never seen. What a shame that men don't have sexes like that!" When the soldiers heard this, they became very excited and eagerly awaited their turn to copulate with her. All the members of the army mounted her, and during the act she lavished love and tenderness on each one. This spurred them to begin again, which they did, and then they left her.[18]

Every time that man is placed in competition with an ass, he loses out. The sexual superiority of the ass over him is deeply embedded in his very genes: "Certain wise men hold that the sperm of the ass always outnumber those of man. In the case of a woman who has copulated with a hundred men and one ass, it is the ass which prevails."[19]

But the ass is not the only invincible conqueror of this voracious vagina. The bear is an especially prized partner of the omnisexual woman, even though he only appears once in the erotic discourse. The rareness of his appearance there is easily explained when one realizes the difficulty that a woman would have in finding a bear in the semiarid areas of the Muslim Near East. Like the first case of the rich young woman with the ass, the lady with the bear is also very rich. It is her butcher who discovers her secret, sumptuously concealed in a beautiful residence in Cairo. The lady with the bear used to buy a lamb every day with such regularity that the butcher became curious, followed her, and caught her in a strange scene of domestic intimacy. He relates:

I slipped into the room and saw that the woman had seized the lamb, cut off the feet which she had put in a pot, and thrown the rest to a bear so enormous that it looked like a camel. I had never seen such a huge one. The bear devoured the lamb. As for her, she poured the contents of the pot, once it was cooked, into some lovely Chinese bowls, ate it until satisfied, as well as fruits and vegetables along with their sauces. She drank from a crystal glass and gave the bear a golden glass to drink from. All this she did until she felt relaxed.

Then she lowered her pantaloons and stretched herself out in front of the bear. It stood up, protruded a penis as large as that of an ass, and copulated with her. She accepted it and talked to it with the same passion that she would have shown to a man in the same circumstances. When it had finished, it settled back, then jumped on her a second time, and so on until it had accomplished the act ten times, and they both lost consciousness and remained motionless for a long time. [20]

The fact that this tale features a bear does not change the essential point of it: the size of the penis. As in the first case related, the whole thing comes to a bad end. Mad with jealousy, the butcher, armed with a very sharp knife, cuts off the head of the beast and proposes marriage to his companion. She refuses the offer and begs him to finish her off too, since life would be unbearable without her beloved. She offers him all her riches as a reward if he will agree to kill her. For her, life would be a torment without the bear, and death a liberation. He cuts off her head and takes possession of her treasure, but not for long. The governor of the city forces him to share it with him as soon as he leaves the strange residence. (The relationship between copulation and money is such a constant theme that it passes unnoticed.)

The animal penis (especially that of certain pachyderms) as the standard and unit of measure by which the omnisexual woman evaluates and sizes up her partners surfaces once again in the tale of a vizir, eager to fathom female sexuality. He asks ten of his concubines to tell him about the most marvelous experience of copulation that they have ever had. Most of them describe the penis of the human partner that they have rated the highest and compare his potency, effectiveness, and especially the size of his member to that of animals.

For one of them, the penis of her human partner resembled the penis of an elephant; for another that of an ass, repeating a now familiar theme. For a third, the resemblance was to a mule. And finally for a fourth, the penis that she loved resembled a suckling kid. [21]

It must already be apparent that the omnisexual woman, moved by the animal force that she has between her legs, can hardly be a good believer, a pious Muslim bound by the faith to be content with one-quarter of a man (Islamic polygyny gives a man the right to divide his favors between four legitimate wives besides innumerable concubines). [22] The unreasonable demands of her voracious vagina are going to compel her to launch an attack on all the rules that govern sexuality in Muslim civilization, and especially those relating to heterosexuality, fidelity, social homogeneity (the social origin of the spouse, the concept of *kafa'*), virtue (prostitution is condemned as the worst possible degradation). And finally these demands will push her to a lack of respect for sex roles.

One of the rules that determines sex roles — the one placing woman in the eternal role of a prey terrified by male desire and ignorant of all sexual technique — represents a legitimated and sacred wish, soothing to the believer in a patriarchal Islam, organized as it is in minute detail to mitigate his feelings of insecurity. This wish is expressed by and incarnated in the myth of the virgin, which occupies a central and constant place in patriarchal Islam. This concept of the virgin is the pole around which sexuality is organized in the Muslim psyche. Neither the trauma of colonization, nor that of neocolonization, seem to have shaken it. Every day young women throughout the Muslim (and non-Muslim) Mediterranean area go to gynecologists' offices to have their virginity artificially restored before their wedding nights. For the omnisexual woman, virginity is obviously an impossible condition. Her desire is a force so irresistible, so biological, so animal that she is fatally impelled to rebel against the constraints, the barriers that are supposed to try to impair her capacity for sexual pleasure. She is by definition in rebellion against all the care taken for hierarchization and classification as the foundation of the spiritual universe of Islam, which is based on the control of biological forces and their subordination to an order designed by and for man and his glorification in the male god, Allah.

It is nevertheless important to remember that never is woman's intellectual ability put in doubt. In the omnisexual universe her capacity for clear thinking is particularly acute when it is a question of destroying the surrounding order. It is not a case of destruction by lack of attention or failure to understand the social import of her acts. In all Muslim discourses without exception, woman is endowed with a particularly keen intelligence that enables her to understand the system and its mechanisms. Her hostility to the system is explicitly destructive because she is fully conscious of her acts and their import. This destructive intelligence has a specific name that the Koran itself has instilled forever in the sacred collective memory of Muslims: the *qaid*, which is a special form of human intelligence. It is female and devoted to the calculated, cold, and permanent destruction of the system.[23] The *qaid* is not a marginal concept worked out by minor authorities. It is a key concept established by the major sources that structure and nourish the Muslim order — the Koran and the orthodox imams — as will be seen in my discussion of the Islamic legal discourse.

# 6  The Omnisexual Woman in Action: Subversion of the Social Order

The author of *How An Old Man Can Regain His Youth Through Sexual Potency* sums up the destructive tidal wave of an omnisexual woman by quoting an important personage of the Mediterranean world, well known for his ambivalence, if not his aversion, toward women — Socrates. When questioned about the virtue of women he is supposed to have said:

> The surprising thing is not that women should fornicate, but that they should be virtuous, because they are creatures whose essence is lust (*al-shawa*). And one of the better proofs of the tryanny of their sexual appetite is the fact that a young woman whose parents have educated her from a young age and cared for her when she is grown up and supervised her, etc., is yet never grateful for all these blessings despite the excellence of her intellect and the sharpness of her mental faculties. She chooses him whom her desire fixes on, and she prefers him to her parents at the very moment when she is fully conscious of her duty toward them and thus of the implications of her actions. . . . There are numerous young women, raised in luxury and wealth and given an excellent education, who desert their native land, exiling themselves in far countries in order to assuage their desires and pursue their quest for pleasure. They do not hesitate in their mad quest to destroy the reputation of their family, to trample on all that is sacred, to soil the family honor, and even sometimes to go as far as murder.[1]

The omnisexual woman is motivated by one sole objective — the pursuit of orgasm, the quest for instruments large enough to calm the convulsions of her private parts. The omnisexual woman is selfish desire incarnate, engrossed only in her own fulfillment and notably lacking a dimension central to the Muslim family, the maternal dimension. For the Muslim family the concern for the perpetuation of the race is paralleled by an equally imperative concern, that of the purity of the race, the guarantee of legitimate paternity. This requires the faithfulness of the wife-mother and her virtue; otherwise the patriarchal design is doomed to failure.

Faithfulness and virtue are not natural for the omnisexual woman. They depend on her willingness to collaborate, her willingness to be self-controlled, to restrain the convulsions of her private parts and impose artificial constraints on her voracious vagina, lined with muscles that vibrate and seek out anything that can satisfy them. The two key roles designed by men to be the pivot of the Muslim family — wife and mother — clash with the essentially biological nature of the omnisexual woman. It is in the light of the omnisexual woman that the

34

wife-mother acquires a particularly unreal focus. She is as much of a fantasy as the veiled, immobilized women behind shutters that Muslim males have nursed as their ideal for centuries. In order to create, using the raw material of the omnisexual woman, a wife-mother fitted for copulation with only her legal husband chosen for her by her wali,[2] it is necessary to immobilize a woman, lock her up, hide her, and separate her as much as possible from the male population.

For although on the level of sexual prowess the ass constitutes an enemy for size, nothing is more devastating for paternity than the sperm of another man. Moreover, another man, having a social existence and being situated in a social hierarchy, could talk and divulge the secrets of the cuckolded husband. An ass, despite the superiority of his sperm, is not capable of that.

Muslim marriage is an exchange of a woman between two men, the wali and the future husband. If such an exchange had to include the opinion of the woman, we would need only the institution of *jabr*,[3] that is, the right of a father to force his daughter to marry the man whom he has chosen for her, to remind us that trust does not exist between father and daughter, that the two do not necessarily pursue the same objective, and that in fact their criteria of choice do not coincide. One of the concerns of the wali (the father or his legal representative) is the question of *kafa'*, social homogeneity.[4]

The criteria that govern the choice of the woman-voracious-crack and those of the wali, who is the representative and guarantor of the Muslim order, can only clash with each other. The criteria that govern the omnisexual's choice can be nothing but a constant source of subversion of the Muslim family. Even more serious is the fact that this source of subversion is endogenous, from within. It is violently intimate, insidiously, tenderly internal to the Muslim family. One imagines the mental maneuvers, so tempting, so easy, which link subversion and femaleness in the shadowy depths of the collective memory. One can imagine the ease with which this link crops up in the present-day crises that the male believer experiences in a society constantly desecrated and assailed from the outside by technology and its masters, and from the inside by the collapse of social hierarchies and the rapid spread of egalitarian ideas.

Femaleness, according to the erotic discourse, is erosion, the leveling of social hierarchies. Femaleness can only assert itself by and through subversion. The wali, the representative of the Muslim order (he is always of the male sex, father, brother, paternal uncle, etc.), in making his choice of the marriage partner for the woman that he represents, has to take into account six criteria that measure *kafa'*. According to Ibn Hanifa, these criteria are: Islam, affiliation, status (free or slave), fortune, profession, and finally *al-tadayun*, conformity of conduct to religious precepts. For a marriage to succeed, there must be homogeneity between the spouses and their families with regard to these six criteria.[5] The concept of *kafa'* is a very obvious breach in the concept of equality among believers, and this explains its ambiguous status and the absence of unanimity concerning it.

This has not prevented it from emerging in the new family-law codes promulgated by the Muslim states after their political rebirth following colonialism.[6] The concept of *kafa'* thus limits the Muslim woman's choice of marriage partners. So it is obvious that this woman would not have the right to exercise any choice concerning sexual partners either inside or outside of marriage. In marriage her sole sexual partner must be her lawful husband; outside of marriage, she must refrain.

Not only does the omnisexual woman exercise the privilege of choice of sexual partners, but she also shows scant respect for the criteria of the males who govern her and make use of her before and during marriage. The omnisexual's sole criterion in her choice of partner is the size of the phallus. It is a criterion that is related to biology, to pleasure. The man-wali's criterion in making his choice is *kafa'*, homogeneity, a criterion related to social, cultural, and religous concerns. The woman's purpose relates to nature; she stands in opposition to culture, to patriarchal, hierarchized, and hierarchizing Islam. By listening to the muscles that throb between her legs, the woman erodes the social hierarchy, opens her vagina to the large phalluses of men of low estate, whom the social order places at the bottom of the social scale, thus effecting a reversal of values:

> Women are demons, and were born as such;
> No one can trust them, as is known to all; . . .
> They do not recoil to use a slave in the master's absence,
> If once their passions are aroused, and they play tricks;
> Assuredly, if once their vulva is in rut,
> They only think of getting in some member in erection.[7]

Writers give many illustrations of the threat to the system represented by woman as a permanent pole of destabilization and subversion of the social hierarchy. Marriage between paternal cousins, regarded as the ideal and preferred by fathers, is an almost sacred union. It guarantees the purity of the bloodline as well as the cohesion of the group and the preservation of its wealth. It was this marriage that a young widow, belonging to a powerful family of rich merchants, chose to profane by copulating on the tomb of her barely interred husband, as related by the author of *How An Old Man Can Regain His Youth Through Sexual Potency.* Her decision to do this was made on the spur of the moment when she saw the size of the penis of one of the blindmen whom she had hired to do the daily ritual reading of the Koran:

> As for me, I come from a rich family of merchants. I was brought up in wealth and luxury. When I was grown up, my father married me to my paternal cousin, who took me and deflowered me on my wedding night. I remained with him for two years, at the end of which he fell ill. Then he died. I was deeply affected by this loss. I even thought about suicide. The death of my husband deeply saddened me and plunged me into mourning. I had a beautiful tomb built for him surrounded

by a large building, and I hired five blindmen to assure regular readings of the Koran on his tomb — readings which were to continue night and day. I passed most of my time at the tomb. I went out one morning at dawn and headed for the tomb. As I drew close to it, I saw one of the hired blindmen asleep, stretched out on his back, his sex in the air, erected like a rod or a well-shaped shaft. My first reaction was one of fear. I cursed the devil and started to waken the blindman. Then the devil changed my mind. The place was deserted, the sex of the blindman in full erection was of a prepossessing size which gave joy to my heart. So without further hesitation I went up to the blindman. I uncovered his sex completely. It displayed itself there beneath my eyes like a vigorous well-fed little animal. At the sight of it, my heart became flooded with desire, and I took off my pantaloons. I moistened the sex of the blindman with saliva and put a little on the lips of my own. Then I inserted the whole of his sex into my vagina, and I felt an enormous pleasure. I began to move up and down on him. The blindman remained motionless and silent. As my excitement grew, I began to taunt him: "Are you made of stone or are you dead?" I shouted at him. "May Allah make you ugly if you do not help me." When he heard me, he took his hand out of his pocket, pulled me down onto his chest, and forcefully thrust himself into me with more and more rapid movements. He took me ten times that day. I left the way of God on that day to devote myself to prostitution.[8]

The idea that the cause of prostitution is the great sexual appetite of women and not the economic structure is a strongly rooted and still enduring belief and occasionally turns up even in studies and essays that call themselves scientific.[9]  It is the throbbing convulsions of a demanding vagina that drive a woman to open up what should normally be reserved for a single man (her husband) to all the members of the community without distinction or the least discrimination. However, the most serious aspect is not that the sexual act undermines the social hierarchy, but that it reverses it: Slaves become masters. In the preceding account, the woman, who belonged to the upper class, was in control during the copulation; she was in the position of authority over the blindman. It was she, the rich woman, who gave the orders; the blindman, a poor man, obeyed her to the letter. In the following account, the dynamics are different. One sees through the eyes of the young dumbfounded narrator a scene of copulation, unbelievable to his eyes. He watches as a woman of free estate, whom he has seen adulated, surrounded, and loved by rich and powerful men whom she scorns, humble herself before a black slave whose penis fascinates her:

I saw a young woman all excited with a black slave. She kept kissing his cheeks and licking them. He, on the other hand, pushed her away, insulted her, and even hit her. She raised her legs in front of him and sobbingly told him the torments she was suffering due to the great passion and tenderness she felt for him. The slave merely insulted her: "Whore," he said over and over. "Master," she kept on replying to his attacks, "do with me what you will. Just stop these attacks and put it in me. I have been away from you for three whole nights." "I will only take you if you do

what you are in the habit of doing," he told her. "With pleasure," she answered.
I was invisible in the shadow, and they were in full light. I wanted to see what this
"habit" of hers was that the slave spoke of. He stood up, his sex in an erection that
was a whole head longer than an arm. She grabbed it, kissed it more than twenty
times, caressed it with her cheeks and wiped her eyes with it. He indicated to her
to stop. During this whole time she kept behaving seductively with sighs and moans.[10]

Indeed, there seems to be a veritable plot to subvert the Muslim order and
its hierarchies and to destroy its institutions — a plot between the omnisexual
woman and the men of low estate, especially slaves, who are invariably in these
cases black:

We negroes have had our fill of women,
We fear not their tricks, however subtle they may be.
Men confide in us with regard to what they cherish.
This is no lie, remember, but is the truth, as you know.
Oh, you women! for sure you have no patience when the virile member
    you are wanting,
For in the same resides your life and death;
It is the end and all of your wishes, secret or open.
If your choler and ire are aroused against your husbands,
They appease you simply by introducing their members.
Your religion resides in your vulva, and the manly member is your soul.
Such you will always find is the nature of women.[11]

This poem by the black slave Dorérame was an answer to the woman Full
Moon of the Full Moon, whom he was pursuing with his desire, a woman
belonging to the masters, wife of the son of the vizir. The stanzas of the dialogue
between the two of them were exchanged in the hearing of the king, powerless
to act in the situation because he was hidden. Strange circumstances had placed
him in the position of voyeur. It was not, however, the words of the slave that
shocked the king the most; it was those of Full Moon of the Full Moon, so
unexpected, so clear, so unamibiguous in their lucidity:

Oh, men! listen to what I say on the subject of woman,
Her thirst for coition is written between her eyes.
Do not put trust in her vows, even were she the Sultan's daughter.
Woman's malice is boundless; not even the King of Kings
Would suffice to subdue it, whate'er be his might. . . .
The wife receives the slave in the bed of the master,
And the serving men allay upon her their lust.[12]

Eventually the king was able to come out of his hiding place and command
Full Moon of the Full Moon to identify for him the women who frequented
the house of debauchery accidentally discovered by him and who were drawn

there by the phallus of Dorérame, the black slave who had a member "stiff as a pillar."[13] The list reflected the whole ruling class of the realm:

"This is the wife of the *Kadi.*" "And this one?" "The wife of the second Vizir." "And this?" "The wife of the chief of the *Muftis.*" "And that one?" "The Treasurer's."[14]

Figuring also in the list were the wife of the syndic of carpenters, the daughter of the clerk of the treasurer, the daughter of the inspector of weights and measures, the daughter of the keeper of the colors, and finally (how symbolic!) the daughter of the guardian of the royal portals — that is, the one responsible for the security of the palace.[15]

This story by Nefzawi (who wrote his work on the order of a vizir) ended not with the women being put to death, but with the killing of the black slave, who was mutilated by order of the king before his execution:

They cut off his ears, nose, and lips; likewise his virile member, which they put into his mouth, and then hung him on a gallows.

Then the King ordered the seven doors of the house to be closed, and returned to his palace.[16]

In the discourse of the marvelous, the black slave who copulates with the daughter or wife of the master is systematically and brutally punished.[17] In the erotic discourse this is not always the case; the slave can sometimes copulate with the women of the master with impunity. This marks a great difference between the erotic discourse and the discourse of the marvelous.[18] It must be noted that rarely in either of these discourses are the women of the powerful punished for fornication or adultery, contrary to the provisions of the law in the legal (orthodox Sunni Islamic) discourse, which demands that the two criminals receive the same penalty.[19] Although in other discourses men of low estate (slave or poor) are punished if they dare desire and possess the women of their masters, it is not always so in the erotic discourse, where men and women succeed most of the time in fornicating with impunity. In the discourse of legal (orthodox) Islam, the body — of women and also of men — is the field on which the writing of power, of authority, of hierarchy is inscribed with the most violence. In the erotic discourse it is a field where the only writing is that of pleasure. Pleasure is the organizing principle of the world, of beings and their relations. It is the order itself, emanating from and situated in female desire.

In erotic space, which is the space of male fantasy par excellence, men of low estate, endowed with cosmic phalluses, can let themselves be tempted by women belonging to powerful men, without undergoing the fate of Dorérame, who, it must be admitted, overdid it a bit and was not satisfied with just one transgression.

A happy fornicator of erotic space was Bahloul, the court fool of a king named Mamoum. He "amused the princes and Vizirs," who "consider[ed] him as a subject for mockery."[20] His great poverty was the thing that amused the king and his dignitaries, and they asked him to compose verses on the subject in exchange for gifts from them. Bahloul, ludicrous as he was, succeeded in seducing Hamdonna, thanks to his member, "which stood erect like a column between his thighs." Hamdonna was far from being just anybody: She was the daughter of Mamoum and the wife of the Grand Vizir. Hamdonna "was endowed with the most perfect beauty; of a superb figure and harmonious form. No one in her time surpassed her in grace and perfection. Heroes on seeing her became humble and submissive, and looked down to the ground for fear of temptation, so many charms and perfections had God lavished on her."[21] And Hamdonna, the perfect object of desire and entertainer of powerful men, was in addition "a marvelous singer, with a delicious voice, able to charm the birds out of the trees. No one had ever heard her sing a song without being completely carried away."[22]

And yet, this siren, beautiful, rich, talented, married to a powerful man, was not only seduced but bewitched by Bahloul, the buffoon, ugly and poor:

> O Bahloul! I never saw a more beautiful dart than yours! . . . O member, come into me . . . on the opening of each vulva is inscribed the name of the man who is to enter it, right or wrong, for love or for hatred. If Bahloul's name had not been inscribed on my vulva he would never have got into it, had he offered me the universe with all it contains.[23]

Not only does Bahloul do very well by himself, but he also succeeds in playing a trick on Hamdonna with the unwitting collaboration of her husband, the Vizir.

The omnisexual woman is invariably triumphant in erotic space. She breaks through all social barriers with impunity and successfully erodes the foundations of the sacred institution par excellence — the family. No bulwark can hold out against her, once the barriers of sex have been vaulted. The omnisexual woman desecrates the rule of heterosexuality with the same ease as the rules of social homogeneity. Homosexuality is a game that does not repel her.

According to Ibn Sulayman, wise men are supposed to have explained homosexuality by the fact that contrary to female animals, whose desires obey the rhythm of the seasons and who only feel the desire to copulate in certain periods of the year, women defy the seasons:

> Females of all kinds of animals, it has been noted by the savants, only feel the desire to copulate during a part of the year; human females feel it incessantly throughout the whole year. The practice of fettering animals limits their desire in a certain way and diverts their attention from their sexual parts, while it is unthinkable for a woman's vagina to abstain. Even if a woman marries seven men, as many as

the days of the week, that would not keep her from seeking homosexual contacts in addition, in order to satisfy herself.[24]

This theory about the homosexual woman in also found in Nefzawi. He describes a case in which adulterous women also indulge in homosexuality.[25] Female homosexuality is thus, in their theory, a consequence of male incapacity. Both authors are convinced that it is enough for a woman to find herself face to face with an adequate phallus for her to renounce this practice, which they regard as simply a solution of desperation in most cases. But if one examines closely what Shaykh Nefzawi describes as an adequate phallus, one becomes aware that there is little chance for saving all the women of the community who are compensatory lesbians and for setting them on the right path.

The erotic prowess of the cavaliers whom Shaykh Nefzawi cites as examples, Abou el Heidja, his companion Abou el Heiloukh, and his servant Mimoun, was rather extraordinary. They broke into the palace of a princess who refused to be married, "wore men's clothing, rode on magnificent horses . . . knew how to handle the sword and the spear, and bore men down in single combat."[26] She lived surrounded by a hundred virgins. Abou el Heidja and his companions succeeded in converting that whole crowd of women, accustomed to homosexual activities, to intercourse with men. But at what a price! Abou el Heidja was given the task of "deflowering eighty virgins without ejaculating."[27] It is true that in order to carry out his mission, Abou el Heidja asked for "camel's milk with honey, and, for nourishment, chick-peas cooked with meat and abundance of onions."[28]

*Amazon*

Abou el Heiloukh had to take on an even more perilous challenge. The lesbian princess, who, before changing course, wanted to be certain of what she was going to win in return, told him: "What I require of you is to remain here, in the presence of these women and virgins, for thirty consecutive days, with your member during this period in erection during day and night."[29]

He amazed the princess by finishing his task victoriously. But she had to feed him during the whole operation with the diet that he demanded: "Onions cooked with meat, and, for drink, the juice pressed out of pounded onions mixed with honey." However, as one should have expected, it was the black slave, Mimoun, who surpassed his masters in a domain where the masters seem fatally destined to lose. Not only did he meet the challenge of the princess, who demanded that he copulate "without resting for fifty consecutive days" with Mouna, "who was insatiable as regards coition," but he "kept going on, besides, for ten days longer."[30] His secret: For nourishment he demanded yolks of eggs and bread. At the end of these feats, the heroes got their reward: "These tasks finished, the men took as booty everything in the palace: women, virgins, furniture, and other objects of value as well. Afterwards they divided their loot into equal parts."[31]

The phallus as an instrument for conquest of the world and its riches is a constant theme in this discourse as well as in the legal discourse, which, as we shall see, is centered on the possession of the female body as the model for all forms of possession.[32]

Usually in these discourses the women whom men desire, try to seduce, and win the love of are rich and/or powerful women. The typical woman that man desires is basically one who belongs to the upper class in one way or another. This is very clear in the discourse of the marvelous and is discernible in a number of laws and regulations imposed by the legal discourse. The link between the female body and wealth is a far from ambiguous motif in these cultural discourses. It is women who are the keys to the riches and treasures found in the palaces they inhabit and the gold they display. It is by gorging them with sex that one can get access to their wealth. It is the phallus that is the instrument for the conquest of the wealth of the world, not work. On this point there is perfect agreement between the erotic discourse and the discourse of the marvelous. The creation of wealth is achieved by something other than work in the strictly economic sense. Moreover, it is in the omnisexual universe that one finds a form of selling of the body unthinkable in the legal discourse — male prostitution. The omnisexual woman not only demolishes the social system, its laws, limits, hierarchies, and categories by practicing fornication in all its forms with human partners of both sexes as well as with animals, but she also, in her desire for destruction, goes so far as to reverse the patriarchal order by transforming the male phallus into a commercial object up for sale:

> To the man whom we love we give our vulva, and we refuse it to him we hate. We share our property with the man we love, and are content with whatever little he may be able to bring to us; if he has no fortune, we take him as he is. But, on the other hand, we keep at a distance him whom we hate, were he to offer us wealth and riches.[33]

So it was that the previously mentioned black slave, Dorérame, who "knows no other passions than for coition and good wine" and who "keeps making love night and day,"[34] got the wife of the Grand Vizir to finance his house of debauchery. In another example a rich woman spent her fortune in buying young lovers and disdained men of her own age: "I was a rich woman, living in luxury. I had a large fortune and I worshipped God's creation through very young men. I spent a lot of money on them. I flattered them and gave them the most beautiful outfits."[35]

Those omnisexual women who have no fortune go to work in order to support the lovers whose phalluses they find pleasing. There was the case of a woman married to a handsome Turkish mercenary whom the king decided to castrate because of some offense to him. She loved her husband before his castration, but afterward the situation was unbearable for her. During a trip she made with her husband and his retinue one beautiful moonlit night, she found one of his servants, a young groom, in the act of fornicating with a mule. She caught sight of a penis that at certain moments resembled a "suckling kid," and at others a "fiery young whelp," and at still others assumed the imposing aspect of an enormous "monastery key."[36] After having sampled its charms, the woman got rid of her rich husband and took up prostitution in order to support her lover. She attended the great feasts and offered herself to the highest bidder: "I brought all my earnings back to him. It would have been a pleasure to proffer him my very soul, if he had deigned to ask for it."[37]

And it is this man, desired, loved, adulated by the omnisexual woman, and fashioned in the image of her desires that we must now try to grasp. To what extent does he come close to or differ from reality, from Everyman? What is the relation between the omnisexual woman's male ideal and real men?

# 7 Man as Fashioned by the Omnisexual Woman: Tent-Pole Man[1]

In order to understand better the fundamental contradiction between the universe structured around female desire (the omnisexual universe as conceived by men) and the universe structured around male desire (the patriarchal universe as organized by orthodox Islam), it must be recalled that, in the latter, woman is an object of pleasure intended for the gratification of man. In the patriarchal universe the sexual act is not an act uniting two persons equally endowed with will; it is an act in which a sole human being masturbates with an object, woman, who is often compared to inanimate objects and categorized as a piece of property.

In Verse 14 of Surah III women are put in the category of possessions that tempt men on earth, just like gold, money, horses, and lands.

The unilateral character of the sexual act is clearly stated in Verse 223 of Surah II: "Your women are a tilth for you (to cultivate) so go to your tilth as ye will."

In this surah, the human being is man. Woman is a category whose human dimension is ambiguous. Woman is defined in terms of her function, her relationship to man. As an entity, she is land, she is real estate, she is inert.

The essence of maleness and the essence of femaleness unfold in relation to each other in a three-dimensional space, each having a position, its own dynamics (or lack of it), and a precise mode of conduct that defines it and opposes it to the other in an immutable and determining hierarchical relationship.

Hierarchical Relationship of Male and Female Essences

|  | MALE ESSENCE | FEMALE ESSENCE |
|---|---|---|
| Dimension 1: Position | Vertical | Horizontal |
| Dimension 2: Dynamics | Mobile, animate | Immobile, inanimate |
| Dimension 3: Mode of Conduct | Endowed with will | Lacking will |

In the orthodox discourse, while the mobile, animate man acts vertically in a space that he controls through his will, woman is deprived of will. Horizontal and immobile, she offers herself up to the force that animates the universe, the male force. It is in and by the sexual act that the principle of domination is carried out, that the hierarchical principle, which is the patriarchal universe, is created and maintained. This hierarchy, the domination of man over woman,

44

is only established at the price of the reification of woman: "In order for one category of human beings to dominate another, it must succeed in converting a portion of that society into a commodity, through the medium of an appropriate series of gradations in rank."[2]

In order for power to exist, it is necessary that the dominated person suffer the mutilation of certain attributes previously shared with the dominator. The reification of woman is a necessary condition for patriarchal domination. The idea of property, possession, and sole enjoyment, is only conceivable if the thing possessed is deprived of will and the capacity for counter-power. A human being cannot possess another human being; the idea is absurd.

If the dominance of one human being by another human being is to succeed, it must be justified, legitimated; that is the function and raison d'être of ideology. It is this objective of the patriarchal discourse that will be examined in Part II of this book. But the preceding explanation is necessary as background for a better understanding of the male/female relationship in the omnisexual universe, where this relationship is reversed. In the omnisexual sphere it is man who is inert, and woman who is active. To use the terminology of the hunt, so dear to Al-Akkad, one of the most eloquent theoreticians of modern Muslim patriarchy, she is the pursuer, he is the prey.[3] The power relationship is still there, but the roles are reversed; it is the woman who has a project, and that project is orgasm, in which she invests her will and energy. The man becomes merely an instrument to be pursued.

It is the voracious-vagina-crack woman who is the subject, the force that dominates the scene. Man is the sought-for object; he is reduced solely to what he has that is useful: his phallus, described in great detail. It is through the characteristics of the phallus required by the omnisexual woman that man is portrayed. He is drawn in the image of the desire that justifies his existence. Men are defined by the characteristics of their penis, as demanded by the desire of the omnisexual woman. In the erotic discourse, man is defined in terms of "penis envy," a longing for the penis that the omnisexual woman wants. The world is reversed. The phallus and its needs are not the point of departure for the organization of the universe. It is female desire for the penis that is the organizing principle. And man is defined in relation to the "envy" of (desire for) the penis that she requires for her orgasm.

The penis that men have is not necessarily the one that the omnisexual woman desires, and it is in relation to female desire that the fear of castration is structured. The fear of castration is the fear of not having a penis able to satisfy the omnisexual woman; it is not, as in the Freudian analysis, the male child's fear of being castrated by the father for desiring the mother. Castration fear in the Freudian discourse is a homosexual fear; it is a matter between two men, and the woman is simply an excuse. In the omnisexual sphere, the fear of castration is a heterosexual fear — man's fear of being rejected by woman for having a defective penis, not able to beget the female orgasm.

## MODALITIES OF THE ORGASM
## REQUIRED BY THE OMNISEXUAL WOMAN

The ideal copulation for two partners is one that is crowned with mutual and simultaneous orgasm:

> Those things which develop the taste for coition are the toyings and touches which precede it. . . . Then do all you can to provoke a simultaneous discharge of the two spermal fluids; herein lies the secret of love. . . . And after the enjoyment is over, and your amorous struggle has come to an end, be careful not to get up at once, but with-draw your member cautiously. Remain close to the woman, and lie down on the right side of the bed . . . from the observance of my recommendations will result the pleasure of the woman. . . . God has made everything for the best![4]

Ibn Sulayman confirms this prescription when he reports the answers of Al-Alfiya (whose name is formed from the Arabic word for thousand [alf], the number of men with whom she has copulated) to the following questions put to her by some less experienced women:

> Q: What should a man do to win a place in a woman's heart?
> A: Caresses before copulation, rhythmic movement before orgasm.
> Q: What creates love and understanding in a couple?
> A: Simultaneous orgasm.
> Q: What provokes hate and destroys understanding in a couple?
> A: The opposite of what I just said.[5]

The testimony of a satisfied wife fully agrees:

> I live in the greatest happiness. My bed is a couch of bliss. When my husband and I are together in it, it is the witness of our supreme pleasure; of our kisses and embraces, of our joys and amorous sighs. When my husband's member is in my vulva it stops it up completely; it stretches itself out until it touches the bottom of my vagina, and it does not take its leave until it has visited every corner — threshold, vestibule, ceiling and centre. When the crisis arrives it takes its position in the very centre of the vagina, which it floods with tears. It is in this way we quench our fire and appease our passion.[6]

And finally the man who is the reflection of the omnisexual woman's desire is described and his attributes defined in an ode to the virile man as woman conceives him: radiant with youth, vigorous, endowed with an eternal erection, and having the only intelligence that counts in this world, that of knowing the female body and its requirements:

> I prefer a young man for coition, and him only;
> He is full of courage — he is my sole ambition,

His member is strong to deflower the virgin,
And richly proportioned in all its dimensions;
It has a head like to a brazier.
Enormous, and none like it in creation;
Strong it is and hard, with the head rounded off.
It is always ready for action and does not die down;
It never sleeps, owing to the violence of its love.
It sighs to enter my vulva, and sheds tears on my belly;
It asks not for help, not being in want of any;
It has no need of an ally, and stands alone the greatest fatigues,
And nobody can be sure of what will result from its efforts.
Full of vigour and life, it bores into my vagina,
And it works about there in action constant and splendid.
First from the front to the back, and then from the right to the left;
Now it is crammed hard in by vigorous pressure,
Now it rubs its head on the orifice of my vagina.
And he strokes my back, my stomach, my sides,
Kisses my cheeks, and anon begins to suck at my lips.
He embraces me close, and makes me roll on the bed,
And between his arms I am a corpse without life.
Every part of my body receives in turn his love-bites,
And he covers me with kisses of fire;
When he sees me in heat he quickly comes to me,
Then he opens my thighs and kisses my belly,
And puts his tool in my hand to make it knock at my door.
Soon he is in the cave, and I feel pleasure approaching.
He shakes me and thrills me, and hotly we both are working.
And he says, 'Receive my seed!' and I answer, 'Oh give it beloved one!
It shall be welcome to me, you light of my eyes!
Oh, you man of all men, who fillest me with pleasure.
For you must not yet withdraw it from me; leave it there,
And this day will then be free of all sorrow.'
He has sworn to God to have me for seventy nights,
And what he wished for he did, in the ways of kisses and embraces during all
    those nights.[7]

It is in contrast with this titan of the bed that the antivirile man is seen —
the one whom no omnisexual woman wants. In the omnisexual context, virility
is the ability to satisfy a woman sexually, not economically as in the patriarchal
context (where a man must provide lodging, clothing, and food for the woman:
*nafaqa*).

Know, O Vizir (to whom God be merciful), that men differ from each other in the
act of intercourse, in the size of their member, its thickness, its vigor, its tendency
to go flaccid. He who is held in contempt by women has an extremely small member,
which is soft, slight, and slow to become erect. Women also feel aversion for the

man who ejaculates prematurely, for him who tarries in coming, for him whose chest is heavy to bear, and for him whose croup is unable to press hard on his partner. When such a man approaches his partner, he isn't concerned about her, he takes no pains. He mounts onto her chest, without any love play, without lavishing kisses on her, without arousing her, without having bestowed on her any favors. Then, with difficulty and weariness, he thrusts his dangling member into her. He bobs up and down once or twice, then falls off her breast as if he had overworked. Such a man is of no use to a woman.[8]

In the omnisexual world, men are divided into two classes: the useful ones, the omnisexual men, able to lavish caresses and orgasms endlessly; and the useless ones, those who have difficulty in succeeding in this kind of tournament. So what we want to find out is if the man fashioned by female desire exists in reality or not. Does the omnisexual man exist or is he a male fantasy? If omnisexual men exist, who are they? Do they belong to a specific social group? Are there a lot of them or just a few?

Producing even more anxiety is the question of whether omnisexual status is a given or the result of a process. Is one born or does one become an omnisexual man? So many basic questions in the omnisexual universe where the female orgasm is the organizing principle! For a man, is being omnisexual a destiny or a choice? Are there actions that can be taken to improve one's performance in the sexual domain?

The two works examined here are in fact centered around these questions, and the whole of both books is nothing but an attempt to explore the various dimensions of these questions, to lull the anxiety they arouse in the believer, and to implore the grace of Allah for help in passing, unharmed and without humiliation, through the obstacle course of copulation. The general thrust of these texts is highly optimistic despite the alarming evidence of the enormous gulf between the ideal and the real, between the omnisexual man and the worthy believer. The fact is that, biologically speaking, the average believer is far from being equipped for such a project. Shaykh Nefzawi agrees with Ibn Sulayman:[9] Copulation energizes woman, gives her more strength; on the contrary it weakens man and reduces his reserves of strength.

Know, O Vizir (to whom God be good!) that the ills caused by coition are numerous. I will mention to you some of them, which to know is essential, in order to avoid them. . . . The excessive practice of coition injures the health on account of the expenditure of too much sperm. For as butter made of cream represents the quintessence of the milk, and if you take the cream off, the milk loses its qualities, even so does the sperm form the quintessence of nutrition, and its loss is debilitating. . . . If, therefore, a man will passionately give himself up to the enjoyment of coition, without undergoing too great fatigue, he must live upon strengthening food [special foods which we will hear about further on] . . . [in order to be] protected against the following accidents to which coition may lead.

Firstly, the loss of generative power.

Secondly, the deterioration of his sight. . . .

Thirdly, the loss of his physical strength; he may become like the man who wants to fly but cannot, who pursuing somebody cannot catch him, or who carrying a burden, or working, soon gets tired and prostrated.[10]

So what is to be done? Is the real man completely condemned to a life of failure with the omnisexual woman? Is there not a margin of liberty where the human will can make its appearance, change the course of biology, impose the stamp of human intelligence, and subvert biology in order to be pleasing to the omnisexual woman and bask in her plenitude? The experts' answer to this question affirms the triumph of civilization over "nature," of culture over biology. Real man can go beyond himself and subvert the biological givens, thanks to that which distinguishes him from animals, his intelligence; thanks to science, to the accumulation of knowledge concerning his own anatomy and that of women, and to the development of a strategy for action based on that knowledge.

## SCIENCE IN THE SERVICE OF PLEASURE

The two authors advise the believer to acquire mastery of the situation through the accumulation of knowledge, the scientific approach to the world. First it is necessary to know the female body well and the murmurings of its least desires in order to master the secret of responding to it. This project will then only succeed if man also knows himself, evaluates his good points and his deficiencies, and maximizes his handling of them. In this sense the two books aim to be, and are organized as, scientific treatises. They lay out the problem at the outset by identifying its elements, and then proceed to a synthesis in which information and prescriptions are copiously thrown at the reader to make it possible for him to resolve the problem. It is important to note that where it is a matter of the female body, the authors turn to female sources of information, often to older women having great experience in this matter, like Al-Alfiya, mentioned above.

Their message is pleaure and female desire. Even when the sources are men, their profound intention (contrary to the discourse of the marvelous) is to probe female desire in order to adapt to it. (In the *Arabian Nights* the will that animates the discourse is the will to please the king, male power, and to adapt to his desires.) This veneration of female desire springs from the scientific approach, from the discoveries and explorations that the authors offer to the believer. This is an essentially Muslim attitude. For the Muslim God, there is no contradiction, no break, between prayer and scientific exploration. Exploring the world and human beings and their complexity is the highest form of prayer. In explaining the anatomy of female desire and the way to master male anatomy in order to respond to it, Shaykh Nefzawi and Ibn Sulayman are fully within Muslim orthodoxy, as far as the methodology of their investigation is concerned. It is the subject that is far from being so, because it makes female sexual pleasure the ultimate aim of the thought and action of the believer. And the God of Islam is jealous of the least threat that might distract the attention of this believer, who owes body and soul to Allah. By definition, Islam is submission, submission to the divine will. The most sacrilegious act possible for a believer is to attach himself to someone else, to serve with the same fervor someone other than Allah.

The quest for pleasure in the omnisexual universe shatters the structure of orthodox Islam, which limits all action and subjects all human thought to the service of the divine. It is in this respect that the erotic discourse is subversive; it breaks down the sacred double hierarchy that places God above everything and designates him as the exclusive aim of life on earth. Sexual pleasure is the triumph of both earthly life and the female body. According to Ghazzali, one of the ambiguities of the institution of marriage is that it must allow man to enjoy the female body without that enjoyment interfering with his allegiance to God. Marriage is a borderline institution between two antagonistic and irreconcilable entities — God and woman:

> Among the dangers of marriage [is] the danger inherent in permitted pleasure, the temptation to give oneself up totally to playful bandying with women, to take too much pleasure in their company, to wallow in enjoyment of them. Marriage risks plunging the body and spirit of the believer into day-long and night-long preoccupations which are intrinsically sexual and which thus prevent man from thinking about the Hereafter and preparing for it. It is in this context that one must understand the remark by Ibrahim Ibn Adham, asking God's mercy: "He who becomes accustomed to burrowing between the legs of women will never succeed in achieving anything at all." Ibn Sulayman goes even further and maintains that he who gets married opts for earthly life. This means that marriage impels him to take heed of nought but life here below. There you have set forth the benefits and drawbacks of marriage. Therefore, it would be an error in judgment to decide that, for such and such a man, marriage or celibacy in the abstract is right for him, if one does not take into consideration all the advantages and disadvantages of each of these choices and clearly explain them to him so that he himself can decide with full knowledge of his reason for doing so.[11]

The believer would be tortured and torn forever between God and the Hereafter on one hand, and woman/body/earthly life on the other hand, if a sacred hierarchy did not happen to deliver him from it by degrading the physical component (female body, earthly life) and subordinating it forever to the spiritual component (God, the Hereafter). The female body in patriarchal Islam has to be degraded, objectified, and utilized as an object; it must never hold the attention of the believer or preoccupy his mind beyond a brief, purely utilitarian pleasure, because it constitutes an endogenous pole of dissidence.

When one analyzes the erotic discourse, it appears that the fears of patriarchal power are well founded. The energy spent by the believer in acquiring adequate knowledge about the female body and equipping himself to assuage, satisfy, and serve it, bear a striking resemblance to religious practice, prayer, and the worship that is appropriate to and due to the divine.

## IGNITING FEMALE DESIRE: CARESSES AND POSITIONS

Despite the enormous desire that inflames the voracious-vagina and its incessant quest for the male organ, orgasm is not produced mechanically by the penetration of one into the other. Female orgasm is not a biological given; it is a social project, a process that necessitates knowledge, concentration, and will, that is, the elements of human activity par excellence — work. The quantity and quality of that work are conditioned by the rhythms of the woman's ejaculation, of which there are three different types:

> Know that women are divided into three categories, as far as ejaculation is concerned: the fast ones, the slow ones, and the medium ones. Tall thin women have a fast ejaculation, small plump women a slow one. The woman who has hard jutting nipples ejaculates rapidly; the one who has a short, stocky figure ejaculates slowly. . . .
> The signal of ejaculation in a woman is the movement of her eyes, which narrow until they look like those of a sleepy jerboa. At this moment also the expression on her face freezes. Sometimes she has gooseflesh, her forehead perspires, her limbs go slack, and she modestly avoids meeting the eyes of her partner. Ejaculation is often accompanied in her by shudders, her breathing accelerates, she hides her face and exposes her vagina and presses it to the man when orgasm overtakes her. These are the signs of ejaculation — know them.[12]

These rhythms are fundamental for working out a strategy regarding orgasm, which sometimes imposes discipline and some perilous constraints on a man. For example, certain of these rhythms force a man to control the degree of penetration and to hold back despite his desire for full entry into his partner. For man, the quest for orgasm, far from being relaxation and self-forgetfulness, is an exercise in control, discipline, and vigilance, which are also the attributes of prayer:

> It is said that women are divided into two categories: the *shagra* and the *qa'ra*. If you want to know which category your partner belongs to, you must make a test. Insert your penis into her; if she begins to move and quiver and her eyes close and the pupils disappear, she is *shagra*. In this case you must insert only half of your penis into her. If, however, you see that she remains immobile as if you have not inserted yourself into her at all, then you should plunge it into her totally; you will see that she will begin to smile, to give you love bites, and to move beneath you.[13]

As in religious practice there is a ritual to be respected, but contrary to the divine where the object of worship is an abstraction that has no physical manifestation, the pursuit of the orgasm obliges a man to put on an act and kneel down before the female body and beg for her *reda*, her benediction. This brings to mind the pagan prayer ritual, the ritual of pre-Islamic idolatry. And in the period of the *jahiliya* (pre-Islamic barbarism) the idols often had the bodies of women:[14]

> Know, O Vizir (God be good to you!), if you would have pleasant coition . . . you must first of all toy with the woman, excite her with kisses, by nibbling and sucking her lips, by caressing her neck and cheeks. Turn her over in bed, now on her back, now on her stomach, until you see by her eyes that the time for pleasure is near.[15]

And Ibn Sulayman, more meticulous in his methodology, more the pedagogue, tries to help the believer keep his head in the heat of action by giving him some categories to guide his moves. He lays out for him a veritable catechism of female pleasure:

> The parts of the body which should be kissed are the thighs, the eyes, the lips, the forehead, the hair, the breasts, the inside of the earlobe, the navel, the inside of the vagina, and finally the hips. The parts of the body that should be bitten are the cheeks, the lower lip, the ears. The parts which are sensitive to being lightly tickled by the nails are the soles of the feet and the inside of the thighs. You can allow yourself to beat lightly with your hands the ankles, the outside of the thighs, the arms, and between the navel and the belly, but you must remember that you should only indulge in these kinds of stimulations with a woman who has a slow ejaculation. . . . If, on the other hand, you do this sort of thing with a woman who has a rhythm of fast ejaculation, you risk upsetting her.[16]

If a thorough knowledge of the rhythms and cycles that kindle the female body is indispensable for anyone interested in the pursuit of the orgasm, a detailed and almost maniacal knowledge of the genital apparatus itself is a necessity:

> Know that woman has two holes besides the one that takes in the penis. . . . One is situated lower than the clitoris, and it is through it that the urine flows. There is another situated even lower than that one, and it is through it that the sperm is evacuated. . . . The two holes are close to each other. But while the one through which the urine comes out is visible, the other one is barely so. They are separated by only the width of a thumb. This little hole is important to the extent that he who knows it and knows its function can manipulate it to accelerate the rhythm of the woman's ejaculation. It is enough to caress it very gently with the penis or the finger. Above all, rough and violent movements near it must be avoided. He who knows how to utilize it brings the woman rapidly to orgasm, and thereby attaches her to him and arouses in her a great love for him. On the other hand, he who

ignores this hole and doesn't take the necessary precautions will make himself hated by his partner, especially if he has a very small penis, even if he is as handsome as Joseph.[17]

The man who is not particularly favored by nature, whose organ doesn't come up to the standards of the omnisexual woman, especially as regards its size, must more than anyone else mitigate his limitations by accumulating the necessary information for building his strategy. In addition to the arsenal of kisses and caresses, man must master the technique of the positions for coitus, the art of transforming the duo of the male and female bodies into a mobile and dynamic unity, which takes place in a space-time between the initial desire to copulate and its objective, orgasm. This imposes on man a rhythm that is not his own, that is foreign to him — the rhythm of female pleasure. The erotic undertaking projects man into the arena of female pleasure where he becomes the instrument, contrary to the patriarchal scheme, which as a matter of principle is centered on male desire. The source of expertise on the question of positions likely to satisfy the partner is the testimony of women who have copulated often and with different men — concubines:

Concubines, because they circulate among various men, sometimes having twenty or thirty consecutive masters, have the opportunity to acquire great knowledge on the subject of copulation. They take advantage of their situation to learn different techniques from each partner. He who wants to make inquiries in this domain must oblige a concubine to communicate to him all the techniques that she has accumulated during her career. Usually they will reveal unsuspected angles to you and cause you to hear sensual sounds and moans never heard before.[18]

Al-Alfiya, for example, who seems to have fascinated Ibn Sulayman, imparted to women less experienced than she, who asked her to share her knowledge with them, eleven positions for copulation while lying on the back, six while seated, and ten while lying on the side. She also went into detail about other much more acrobatic techniques, particularly ten positions while squatting and ten others while prostrate.[19] These positions smack of fantasy and humor, and their titles often sound like risqué theater pieces: "The Routine" (Nayk al-'ada); "The Copulation of the Masters" (Nayk al-sada); "The Conformist" (Al-tatabu'i); "Position for a Lazybones" (Nayk al-kasali); "Suggestion" (Al-muqtarih); "The Au-Revoir" (Al-wadaa'); "Copulation of the Specialists" (Nayk al-mukhtassin); "Technique of the Amateurs" (Nayk al-walaa').[20]

But Al-Alfiya's positions suddenly seem very banal when one compares them to those propounded by a concubine who was a specialist in sodomy. Her master recounted that she made him undergo a veritable test when he bought her. When she realized his knowledge about sodomy was rather vague, she got down to the task of seriously initiating him into this art. She cited sixteen positions to him and offered herself as a skilled teacher to guide him in learning them through practice. "The best method of teaching," she told him, "is always action."[21] In the course of the sessions initiating him into these practices, he reported that he had some moments when he was totally overwhelmed, especially with regard to the ninth position: "I wanted to get up. She told me: 'Don't move.' Then she removed my sex from hers with her own hand; she put it into her mouth, began to suck it and manipulate it until it stiffened again."[22]

In these passages concerning techniques and positions, the relationship between master and slave is reversed. The men, trembling with curiosity and anxiety, become the disciples and initiates, and the slaves arrogate to themselves all the rights of intimidating and giving orders that belong to educators. Reading the text leaves you with an aftertaste of anxiety. It seems that the believer is far from having the constitution required to be an omnisexual man. What he can offer his partner doesn't come close to being what will satisfy her. So it becomes necessary for a man to know his limits, which depend strictly and fatefully on his physical constitution. A man must find out what his own rhythm is, otherwise he risks burning himself out, foolishly committing hara-kiri:

> The sage, Es Sakli, has thus determined the limits to be observed by man as to the indulgence of the pleasures of coition: Man, be he phlegmatic or sanguine, should not make love more than twice or thrice a month; bilious or hypochondriac men only once or twice a month. It is nevertheless a well established fact that nowadays men of any of these four temperaments are insatiable as to coition, and give themselves up to it day and night, taking no heed how they expose themselves to numerous ills, both internal and external.[23]

And it is for this reason that Shaykh Nefzawi included in his list of bad women "the one who exhibits herself in front of her husband in order to obtain her pleasure, and who pesters him constantly in bed."[24] In addition, certain positions are not favorable for a man and risk ruining his health forever:

> Coition, if performed standing, affects the knee-joints and brings about nervous shiverings; and if performed sideways will predispose your system for gout and sciatica. . . . Do not mount upon a woman fasting or immediately before making a meal, or else you will have pains in your back, you will lose your vigour, and your eyesight will get weaker. If you do it with the woman bestriding you, your dorsal cord will suffer and your heart will be affected; and if in that position the smallest drop of the usual secretions of the vagina enters your urethral canal, a painful stricture may supervene. . . . Too much exercise after coition is also detrimental. Avoid washing your member after the copulation, as this may cause canker. . . . The excessive practice of coition injures the health.[25]

What an awful comedown, what a huge gulf between the man whom the omnisexual woman celebrates as "full of courage" with a member "strong . . . and hard . . . always ready for action," and this poor puny creature who is exhausted by the merest movement and suffers sciatica, shiverings, and weak eyesight with the least prolonged effort! How is one then to close this frightful gap? What means can one use to try, if not to eliminate it, at least to reduce it? The authors unanimously reassure the believer by opening two avenues of hope — diet and magic. The first makes it possible for him to store up energy with particularly nutritious foods that will give him the strength necessary for copulation and restore the strength that the sexual act burns up. The second will make it possible for him to realize a miracle: to enlarge the penis and lengthen it, to prolong erection for whole nights, to postpone ejaculation, and finally to make the vagina of the beloved woman hermetically sealed and inaccessible to anyone else. Although Shaykh Nefzawi is content to give just a few prescriptions, Ibn Sulayman, whose book is addressed to the old man whose precise wish is to regain his youth through the ability to copulate, gives him 150 minutely detailed prescriptions.

Anxiety about impotence and premature ejaculation and obsession with the size of the penis and means for lengthening and enlarging it are the subjects of entire chapters in standard medical tracts and manuals, which continue to be guides for an impressively sizable audience of believers, judging by their low price and constant presence in bookshop windows and on stands at the entrances to mosques. Al-Suyuti, in his book *Al-Rahma fil-tibb wal-hikma* (Divine Mercy in Medicine and Wisdom), has a chapter entitled "Increasing the Power to Copulate," in which he gives sixty prescriptions, some containing potions capable of "producing a tenfold increase in man's sexual energy to the point of making him capable of copulating without stop for a whole night." Moreover, if one takes these potions continually, "the penis remains full-blown and in constant erection without ever subsiding."[26]

Some of Imam al-Suyuti's other potions are so virulent that, once ingested, they create the opposite problem — that is, the penis will stay in a state of erection "until you run cold water over your organ several times."[27]

Imam al-Suyuti devotes special sections of his book to orgasm (eighteen prescriptions) and to methods for enlarging the penis (ten prescriptions). He offers six prescriptions for reducing a woman's sexual appetite, and fifteen methods for blocking the access of anyone else to the vagina of the beloved woman, and to keep her from fornicating.

Shaykh al-Imam Ibrahim Ibn Abd al-Rahman Ibn Abi Bakr al-Azraq, in his book *Tashil al-manafi' fil-tibb wal-hikma* (Obtaining the Benefits of Medicine and Wisdom),[28] specifies that "man is advised against copulating too much"[29] in a section with that precise title, and then goes on to devote whole sections to means for increasing a man's sexual appetite and strength and for enlarging his penis, and on the other hand to prescriptions for reducing a woman's sexual appetite.[30]

The symbolic content of these prescriptions is as impressive as their number. Most of them depend on the most elementary techniques of magic, such as carrying, touching, or rubbing oneself with the sex organ or other parts of the bodies of animals known for their great sexual appetite or the large size of their sex organs. To increase one's sexual appetite, it is enough to carry around the bile of a bear, or the testicles of a fighting cock, or hair taken from an ass during copulation.[31] Touching the tail of a fox miraculously renews one's energy.[32] Smearing the penis with bear grease, a bull's sperm, the yolk of an eagle's egg, or, better still, a tiger's brain increases the size of the penis and its endurance.[33]

But it is the mouth that is the means most utilized for producing miracles in the field of sexuality. Orality is the key to sexual prowess in a very large number of these prescriptions. For the man who feels himself to be sexually debilitated, swallowing is the act that regenerates his strength and increases his sexual appetite tenfold. Swallowing is the favored act for renewing faltering powers and dangling penises. Having been nourished through the mouth at the time when, as a babe in arms, his energies were only potentialities, man regresses to it when he reaches the limit of his powers. Worried about being able to please the loved one, he returns to the mouth, "the organ of nourishment from the mother." In order to satisfy the voracious-vagina of the omnisexual woman, man has recourse to another orifice, just as devouring of energy, the mouth.

The mature man, who at one moment was intoxicated with his youth and expected to conquer the world (which is in the omnisexual universe, woman) becomes a child again when he has doubts about his capacity, his strength. The child reappears in the man when he is perturbed in his effort to please, in his desire to be loved. Orality can consist of pronouncing a few words that will change the world, that will revive the sleeping penis. Ibn Sulayman advises him who suffers from premature ejaculation to pronounce the following words: "*ach-ach-driath-dith-dith-dathat-dathat*." These words alone will work the magic: The lover will be able to prolong his act as long as he wants to.[34]

Swallowing the sexual organs of other animals results in marvels; the penis of the wolf and hedgehog, the testicles of the fox, the ass, and the cock create miracles.[35] Four items of food, much more banal than the preceding, occupy a favored place in the oral banquet recommended by the *fuqahas* (scholars of religious science): honey, milk, egg, and onion. In a society of scarcity, where rich foods are reserved for the dominant minority, this diet opens the royal road to eternal youth for the kings, vizirs, and those in their entourages, and at the same time bars from it the majority of believers:

> If, therefore, a man will passionately give himself up to the enjoyment of coition, without undergoing too great fatigue, he must live upon strengthening food, exciting comfits, aromatic plants, meat, honey, eggs, and other similar viands. He who follows such a regime is protected against . . . the loss of generative power . . . the deterioration of his sight . . . the loss of his physical strength.[36]

# 8 Conclusion: The Limits of Using the Male As the Source of "Truth" About Female Reality

And so ends the erotic discourse. It dies out in a cry of anguish, the anguish of not being up to the omnisexual task: the pursuit of the orgasm of an insatiable female. This anxiety about failure, this threat of endogenous castration is the just punishment for an unpardonable lapse in behavior — that of the heretic who indulges in the most blasphemous act possible against Islam, polytheism, the act of setting up other gods than Allah as objects of a cult. But even more serious, in this erotic lapse, is the fact that the *fuqahas*, impelled by a diabolical curiosity, are on the side of female desire, of the female will to reconstruct the world. In the erotic discourse, men of good faith, pious imams and shayks, animated by an authentic desire to strengthen the community, committed a mortal sin: probing female desire. It was an aberration that led them along unknown paths.

The erotic discourse is heretical in that it is animated by the desire to explore the inferior, the subordinated, the oppressed, the repressed, the excluded. Orthodox legal methodology prescribes investigating only the will of God, the will of the master, never that of slaves. The Imams Nefzawi and Ibn Sulayman disregarded Allah's limits; they overstepped the boundaries that restrict human curiosity and limit what may be subjects of interest, investigation, and knowledge. They took an illegitimate subject as their subject of study, and, just as dumbfounded as their readers, they exhumed from the depths of repressed memory the fossilized traces of the *jahaliya* (the period of pre-Islamic barbarism), a world of reversed values and upset equilibriums, where women slaves were masters and their masters were slaves. They evoke a universe shaped to the rhythm of female desire, where man is fragile and women strong. They evoke a universe where the vagina is the center of incessantly renewed energy, and the penis is weak and powerless. It is the man who is dying of penis envy, a female penis such as the omnisexual woman wants.

The Muslim men of science, Shaykh Sidi Muhammad Nefzawi and the "savant of the century, unique in his time," Mawla Ahmad Ibn Sulayman, probably did not realize that in embarking headfirst (or phallus-first) upon the exploration of female desire, they were going to come out castrated. The man who makes the erotic voyage with them comes out with a problematic penis that has to be nourished, fattened, and smeared with energizing balms to keep it in a state of permanent erection, the one and only position fit for a man in the

57

presence of the omnisexual woman. Any other position, any other posture of the phallus is a complete and total failure. A man is a phallus in constant erection or he is not a man.

Pleasure, the temple of peace and quiet, idleness, and relaxation, becomes a genital prison where man, reduced to his sexual organ, can exist only when it is in a state of erection and able to satisfy a woman who is herself reduced to being a vampire-vagina. Having entered the temple of desire to find pleasure, our savants came out mutilated, and their mutilation is genital. For in real life there doesn't exist a man, especially after a certain age, having a phallus in constant erection, except in the realm of fantasy. Furthermore, in order to achieve this phallus-man, it is necessary not only to reduce man to his genital organ, but also to reduce all of reality to genital existence. This is the fundamental characteristic of the erotic discourse: Human beings who parade through that universe are deprived of their political and economic dimension; they are not seen confronting nature to extract its vital wealth and oversee the distribution of it in order to insure the survival of a group. The "reality" of the erotic universe is a "reality" reduced to the genital dimension, where men and women invest their energy in and are animated by one sole objective, genital pleasure in the narrowest meaning of the term; namely, a series of almost mechanical contacts between two fetishized bodies reduced to their material dimension of limbs, breasts, vagina, and phallus, where orgasm, the crowning result, revolves around and is linked to a process itself mechanical: erection. The dictionary defines *mechanical* as an adjective relating to or concerned with machinery or tools (the opposite of thinking, of intelligence).

The erotic discourse then has two kinds of destructive impacts. The first is on the environment, and the second on the human body, since the body and its environment are inevitably linked and mirror each other. In the human environment, the erotic discourse wipes out all the areas of life that link an individual to his environment (particularly the political area, the quest for power over others) in order to constrain and imprison that individual in one sole area, the sexual area. But this sexual area, which should include a gamut of human interchanges, especially intellectual, affective, and bodily interchanges, is reduced to simple genital manipulation through the elimination of other potentialities of the human body.

The woman and the man who are the subjects of the erotic discourse are beings whose initial bodily makeup, characterized by a multiplicity of elements and faculties, has been cruelly betrayed and reduced to its genital apparatus in the narrowest sense, for the citizens of the erotic universe are sterile. In no case do they concern themselves with reproduction, pleasure being their one and only objective and end. But this end, this pleasure, although it claims to be an investigation, an exploration of female desire, is an exclusively male endeavor and experience. The erotic discourse is female desire as mirrored in men's thought. It is the idea of female desire and pleasure formed by Shaykh Nefzawi and Mawla Ahmad Ibn Sulayman, which they take as the point of departure of their investigation for depicting the man desired by woman. This male exploration of the female world becomes an invasion, since the person inhabiting that world, woman, is violated in her humanity and reduced by the force of conquering male knowledge to a sterile but omniscient genital apparatus. The male explorer, conquering by the very method of investigation that he has chosen, namely, projection on another and not communication with her, has set himself up as conqueror. This projective method replaces the will and opinion of the person being investigated with that of the investigator. The information gathered by Nefzawi and Ibn Sulayman described desire and pleasure as they directly experienced it or as it was recounted to them by a male transmission belt, even when the source was female. Is it because the Muslim savants, who decided to investigate desire and pleasure, deliberately locked themselves into male subjectivity that the erotic world they created and the beings that people it are mutilated, reduced, impoverished, and suffering from cruel amputation of their faculties? Not only the person investigated but also the investigator ends up fatally mutilated as a result of this kind of investigation, based on projecting the male vision onto the world and human beings, instead of communicating and listening, which would have produced a multiplicity of visions, or at least a duality of visions, a female vision and a male vision.

From the world of desire seen exclusively through male subjectivity spring a man and a woman with deformed and cruelly disfigured bodily makeups, reduced to being automatic vagina and phallus, where the human is liquidated in favor of a solely genital organism.

It will now be interesting to compare these vagina-women and phallus-men, citizens of the world of pleasure as conceived by the Muslim savants of erotic science, with the citizens of the universe of legal Islam, orthodox Islam, the universe of law and power, which has as its objective, laid down as a sacred end, the development of spirituality, the expansion of the sacred, whether in the world or in human beings.

# PART II
# THE ORTHODOX DISCOURSE:
# THE FEMALE BODY AS THE PRODUCT
# OF MALE SACRED POWER

# 9 The Female Body
## As a Field of Sacred Writing

Every discourse re-creates the world and fashions it according to its priorities and ends. Every discourse re-creates the body, whether female or male, according to its priorities and ends. What we want to see is how the female body emerges as a field of cultural writing in the orthodox Islamic discourse. There are several interesting reasons for comparing the erotic discourse and the orthodox discourse as separate and distinct writings on the female body as a cultural field.

The first is that the orthodox Islamic discourse is defined as the discourse of spirituality, a dimension totally absent from the erotic discourse. The latter occupies itself solely with pleasure in the "here and now," and the bodies that it brings into play are fetishized entities, reduced to their material, physical dimension, and carefully stripped of all intellectual and affective dimensions. On the other hand, orthodox Islam is a vision that proposes to spiritualize matter, to give it a scope that transcends the finite in order to attain the infinite. The ultimate aim of life, in the orthodox Islamic discourse, is the infinite, the Hereafter, Paradise, the very incarnation of the spiritual. Paradise, the Hereafter, does not exist materially for a sojourner of this earthly life. He is obliged to project himself, with the aid of his imagination, beyond the limits of the physical world in order to understand the spiritual ends that must motivate him — the Hereafter and access to Paradise. Orthodox Islam, as a social project, subordinates the material to the spiritual. As a strategy for civilization, the spiritual is the objective of human life and its justification. So we are confronted with a discourse fundamentally opposed to the erotic discourse. In the latter the material has no objective other than itself and only comes into play by falling back upon its like, another body. The objective of the erotic discourse is physical pleasure, and it thus limits itself to the body as a material field. The erotic is the quest for pleasure of one body through another body. There is no pretention of going beyond the physical. The woman of the erotic discourse is exclusively a physical apparatus; better still, her whole body is absorbed into an overpowering vagina that is her preeminent feature. What we want to find out is whether the orthodox discourse, so fundamentally different from the erotic discourse because of its spiritual dimension, will produce a female body different from the one manipulated by the erotic discourse.

The question to be answered is whether in the orthodox discourse the female body will be spiritualized, that is, designed for a destiny that transcends the physical and material in order to reach a spiritual end that would conform to the Islamic strategy for civilization. If the female body, as the cultural product of a sacred vision of the world, emerges as an exception to the spiritualization

63

of the material and physical, one can then ask why this is true. Why does Islam, whose purpose is to give a spiritual dimension to the material, refuse this dimension to women? This fact in itself will be the bearer of a very significant message.

We have seen in the erotic discourse how our shaykhs and savants, having embarked on an inquiry into pleasure, were castrated along the way by setting up the vagina, which had to be the source of pleasure, as a devouring and devastating force. They ended up their exploration of pleasure and its spaces with a pitiable, problematic penis that had to be nourished and annointed with balms, massaged, and energized with magical symbols to be able to accomplish the unique task that justifies man's existence: erection. Having at the outset reduced the female body to an atrophied genital apparatus, they found themselves with a male bodily makeup just as disfigured, atrophied, and diminished, where sex, stripped of intellectual and affective elements, is reduced to only the genital. What then is the approach of the orthodox discourse to the body, both male and female? How does the orthodox Islamic discourse interpret the female body? Is the female body in the orthodox discourse a body with multiple dimensions and potentialities, intellectual, affective, and physical? Or rather does this discourse make excisions of one kind or another on this body? If the answer is yes, what is excised and to serve what purpose? Is the female body, as it is produced in the orthodox Islamic discourse, fetishized or spiritualized?

The second difference between the religious erotic discourse and the orthodox Islamic discourse is that the former is the work of human beings while the latter is the creation and manifestation of a divine force, of a god. As a result, the two messages have a different import: The erotic discourse has an individual import, and the orthodox Islamic discourse has a collective import.

Contrary to the religious erotic discourse, which is a simple investigation of the mystery of pleasure, the orthodox discourse sets itself up as legislator, as source of law, as engineer of social order, as architect of reality.

The erotic discourse belongs to the realm of the marginal, the individual; the orthodox discourse is situated, on the other hand, in the realm of power, legitimacy, dominance, and the collectivity. And it is this point that makes the comparison between the two so interesting. The orthodox discourse, source of truth and laws that guide the actions and thoughts of the believer, is not the work of humans; it is the work of a supernatural force who is God the creator, guardian, and master of the group. The orthodox discourse is the discourse of power. It is not simply a discourse on power; it is power. It is as such that it sets up the universe and organizes its elements and gives them their values in a global system of precise signs and messages — that of the Muslim cultural order.

Asking what is the link between the sacred and the sexual is a misconceived way of questioning the religious construction of reality, since these two fields govern the same thing, human life, and are the two most striking expressions of it. If the sexual is the impulse that gives birth to life, the sacred is also, in its way, an impulse that gives birth to life, as we shall see.

The difference between the two is in their relationship to expression, to discourse. While the sexual gives birth to life in the world of reality, since women give birth every day and thus reproduce the human race, the sacred gives birth to life through and in discourse. While the sexual functions at the level of material acts, the sacred functions at the level of the word, the abstract, at the level of perception and representation. The sacred is, among other things, a discourse about sexuality, but with this characteristic: It denies to sexuality the giving of life, which it claims as its exclusive attribute.

The relationship between the sacred and the sexual is then a power relationship: The sacred devours the sexual in order to reproduce it at the level of discourse. In the Muslim universe there is no purely sexual field; there is only a regulated sexual field, coded and systematized according to the options and priorities of Islam as a culture and a strategy for civilization.

What interests us here is not the difference between the sexual and the sacred as fields of human activity, because, as will soon be seen, Muslim civilization as a cultural order takes over reality in order to transform it in discourse. And this transformation of reality into discourse is not accompanied by the disappearance or alteration of this reality, but simply by an imposition of discourse on reality. The discourse of the sacred on sexuality coexists with the sexual as determined by the physical, material order. You have on one side an idea, paternity, the Islamic discourse on the sexual, and this is the affiliation that decides that the child belongs to the father. On the level of material reality, you have on the other side the woman who gives birth to the child. The material reality and the sacred discourse peacefully coexist, even though they are in flagrant contradiction. The cultural reality is precisely this miracle, which ensures that a given dominant discourse is coherent and intelligible, even though it is belied by the facts. And the sacred discourse perfectly illustrates and incarnates culture as the rewriting of reality.

Since our aim is to decode the messages that the orthodox discourse writes on the female body, what interests us is the game of mirrors and reflections that the sexual and the sacred play with each other. Central to our aim is discovering the precise relationship, the interplay between the material and the ideological, deciphering the messages that the sacred, the ideological, imprints on the material — in this case, the female body. On the level of reality, the only being who gives life is the female being, and the sole element able to create and maintain that life is material nature, the flora and fauna, the ecology. However, the sacred explicitly dispossesses both woman and nature of their capacity to create life and maintain it.

The sacred also constitutes a programmed and harmoniously balanced two-pronged attack (and this is where its force and potentialities lie in the twentieth century): On one hand, by the ideological against the material, that is, of the abstract against concrete nature; and, on the other hand, by the male principle against the female principle. In both cases, it is an attack and seizure of power by the party that neither engenders nor nourishes against the party that does both. It is also an attack of the imaginary against the material, of abstract thought against the concrete.

And in this attack of the ideological against reality, sexuality (with all its component parts and with the female body as a central component) plays a fundamental and indispensable role. The role that falls to sexuality in the realm of the sacred (as the ideological appropriation of reality) is so decisive and determining that if one changed it, the whole Muslim order would collapse.

The existence of God is rooted in the very existence of man. And man cannot reproduce himself; it is a woman who reproduces him. So the existence of God necessarily entails the confiscation of woman's ability to engender and give life.

The universe of orthodox Islam is modeled around a pivotal relationship that gives a structure to heaven and earth, to Paradise and fleeting life, and that animates the movement of the stars, the winds, the seasons; it is the relationship between God and the believer. It is the reason for existing in the world here below and in the Hereafter. Everything revolves around that relationship in one way or another, and nothing has meaning except with regard to it. And so it is with regard to that fundamental relationship that the relationship between the sexes must be understood and analyzed. The latter emerges in the Muslim cosmology as a faithful reflection of that basic relationship in which one of the parties is wholly subject to another.

The connection between the divine being and the human being varies according to sex. The divine being in his programming of the universe set up two distinct relationships, each of which conforms to a very specific code. The relationship of the Muslim God to man is not only different from the one he maintains with woman, but her relationship to man is only understandable through an analysis of the triangular relationship between God, the male believer, and the female believer.

The relationship of love between the divine and the human is inscribed in a precise relationship to time and space. It is a relationship in which one of the parties, the divine being, has complete mastery of time and space, the two components of action and thus of power, and the other party, the human being, is fatally bereft of it. The mastery of time and space, the manifestation of divine power, is at the same time the incarnation of human impotence. The two parties, the divine and the human, are bound together in a relationship of inversion in which the affirmation of the one signifies the weakening of the other, in which the triumph of the one inevitably signifies the defeat of the other. This inversion-linkage, which freezes the two elements in a hierarchized relationship of inequality and conflict, is the key schema that animates all the elements of creation and programs their interaction. This inversion-linkage is the code that programs the interaction of elements from the time they enter into relationship with each other, and this relationship is always predetermined. There is no chance relationship in the sacred construction of reality. The elements of creation can only be conjugated according to a rigidly codified sacred grammar. As will be seen further on, this explains the phobic attitude of Islam toward change, *bid'a* (innovation), condemned as one of the most serious of heresies.

Since the programming and codification is the work of the divine will, any upsetting of this program, of this sacred code, is a direct attack against God, who orders and orchestrates all movement.

It is around an affective notion, worship (*al-'ibada*), that Islam is built as a cultural order. The affective is the keystone of the system, and it is structurally linked to the economic realm.

In the orthodox Islamic discourse, the believer is obliged to worship God, and God in reward guarantees him access to material riches. The affective and economic realms are thus interconnected in a binding relationship.

It is through an analysis of the "love" relationship between God and his subjects that one can understand how irrelevant is the dividing line that people try to set up between the sexual and the sacred on one hand and the sacred and the economic on the other. The analysis of this love relationship will show us how negligible are certain distinctions in the sacred realm that are pertinent to analyses of the profane realm. These could be listed as follows: the distinction between the economic and the domestic (the latter being defined as noneconomic), the distinction between the sexual and the political (the sexual being regarded as outside the political field), or even the distinction between the economic and the affective (the affective being perceived as untranslatable into economic terms).

We are going to trace the outline of this structural code, this inversion-linkage, through the systems of relationships in two fundamental areas of life:

1. The ecological field, the universal theater where the actions of living beings take place, especially sacred time and space. Sacred time is not profane time. We will see how time is used as the apparatus of power. We will see how sacred time and sexuality are combined to construct the universe as a structure of inequality.

   Sacred space is not profane space. We will analyze the economic field, the space where the process of work and the creation of wealth take place. We will see how sacred space and its wealth are combined with sexuality to construct the universe as a structure of inequality.

2. The domestic field, the space where the process of the reproduction of human beings takes place, which is defined as being the only field where the relationship between the sexes, driven out of the other two, is actualized.

We are going to see that the relational schemas that operate at the heart of each of these fields, as well as the relationship of the two fields with each other, are identical to the key schema between the divine and the believer, that is, the relationship of domination, which we are calling inversion-linkage. Inversion-linkage ties two elements (here God and the believer) in a relationship of dependence structured in such a way that any attempt by the dominated element to reestablish equilibrium is perceived as opposition, subversion, and questioning of the existing hierarchy. The inversion-linkage that structures the rapport between God and believer reflects and is reflected in the relationship between the sexes. The code that governs the relationship between man and woman in the domestic field, far from being an exception, is the same rule that regulates beings and elements in the sacred system. The systematic hierarchization, the inversion-linkage that governs the domestic field and subjects the party who creates in actuality (the woman, who gives birth and reproduces human beings) to him who does not give birth (man), is the same systematic hierarchization that in the economic field governs the rapport between him who creates wealth by and in the process of work (the human being) and him who appropriates it (the divine being). And these two fields, the domestic and the economic, do nothing but echo and reflect the basic code that splits the structure of the universe into two spaces and time sequences — life on earth and Paradise.

# 10 The Ecological Field: Universal Inequality and Sexual Inequality

The distinction between the sexes and the relationship of domination between the male believer and the female believer are far from being atypical or marginal in Islam. On the contrary, they are a fundamental formulation that supports, reflects, and is reflected in the construction of the Muslim universe.

The sacred universe is organized along anatomical lines. All beings, whether divine, human, or other (with barely one exception), have a specific sex. (The exception is angels, about whose sex a certain degree of ambiguity prevails.) Segregation by sex operates, first, as a mechanism of destruction, and then, as a mechanism of hierarchization in three applications of power: discourse, time, and space.

## THE SACRED DISCOURSE AS GENERATOR OF MALE POWER: DISCURSIVE PRACTICES AND ANATOMICAL GIVENS

What we want to discover is how discourse and sex are interconnected in the field of the sacred. But first we must identify who the beings are who coexist in the sacred field before looking at the relationships between them.

In the sacred universe, concrete beings, human and animal, represent only one category among others. There are three categories of abstract beings: the category of the divine, the category of angels, and the category of spirits. Except for the category of angels, all the categories are defined anatomically as belonging to either the female or male sex. Moreover, the sex of angels seems to have been one of the subjects that preoccupied human beings, a preoccupation deemed presumptuous by the divine being:

> 27. Lo! it is those who disbelieve in the Hereafter who name the angels with the names of females.
> 28. And they have no knowledge thereof. They follow but a guess, and lo! a guess can never take the place of the truth.
>
> (Surah LIII, "The Star")[1]

We will return to these verses later on when we take up the attitude of the divine being toward the family and the process of reproduction in general.[2] For the moment we will simply note that humans attributed female sex to the angels, and that the divine being disputed their point of view. It is not important for us here to debate the sex of angels or try to determine it, but it is important to be aware that the sex of beings assumes a particular importance for the sacred organization of the universe. It is one of the key differences and plays a determining role in the application of power in the sacred construction of reality.[3]

In the field of the sacred it is the religious discourse that organizes the world and sets up its relationships. It is the source of truth and legitimacy, and thus of power. The religious discourse is the world's order. And it is the monopoly of the divine being, who is of the male sex. He addresses human beings indirectly through intermediaries, who are privileged human beings, the prophets. They are without exception also of the male sex:

> 7. And We sent not (as Our messengers) before thee other than men whom We inspired.
>
> (Surah XXI, "The Prophets," p. 420)

Since the transmitting of the religious discourse was a monopoly of the male sex, we are prompted to ask what took place at the receiving end. Did the divine being and his prophets address women, or were women invisible as auditors and thus reduced to being the object of religious discourse?

This question did not escape the attention of two religious authorities, two qadis known for their great intellectual rigor, Ibn al-Khatib and Ibn Khaldun. Ibn Khaldun was in agreement with Ibn al-Khatib, whom he cited on the fact that the divine being only addresses his orders to him who has the power to execute them:

> God . . . only addresses his order to him who has the power to carry it out. Haven't you noticed what Ibn al-Khatib said about women? The majority of religious laws are not addressed to women. Women are not mentioned in the discourse. Nevertheless these laws apply to them as they apply to men. According to Ibn al-Khatib, women are included by analogy (bil-qiyas). Laws are not addressed to them because they are without power. It is men who control their acts, save in regard to the acts of worship properly speaking (al-'ibada). For these acts, women are directly mentioned in the discourse; they are not included there by analogy.[4]

So there are two modes of sacred discourse regarding women. The first is that in which woman is directly mentioned in the discourse, where she is addressed by name; it relates to acts of worship where men and women are on a level of equality before God:

> 30. Tell the believing men to lower their gaze and be modest. . . .
> 31. And tell the believing women to lower their gaze and be modest. . . .
>
> (Surah XXIV, "Light," p. 460)

2. The adulterer and the adulteress, scourge ye each one of them (with) a hundred stripes. And let not pity for the twain withhold you . . .

(Surah XXIV, "Light," p. 456)

40. . . . whoso doeth right, whether male or female, and is a believer, (all) such will enter the Garden, where they will be nourished without stint.

(Surah XL, "The Believer," p. 622)

In these verses the divine being maintains, through his discourse, an identical and rigorously symmetrical relationship toward believers of the male sex and believers of the female sex, whether by addressing the two of them directly (Verse 40 of Surah XL and Verse 2 of Surah XXIV) or indirectly through his prophet (Verses 30 and 31 of Surah XXIV).

The symmetry that marks the relation of the believers of different sexes to the divine in these instances is reflected in their appearance by name in the linguistic structure of the text. One has thus the following linguistic schema:

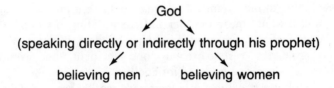

In the second mode of sacred discourse regarding women — that concerning religious laws, in other words, the organization and management of Muslim society — women disappear at the level of discourse, even when it is a question of laws where they are directly involved, such as those regarding marriage. In this second mode, the divine being speaks to men directly or indirectly (through the prophet) about rules and laws that men must respect vis-à-vis women. In this mode women are reduced to the status of background figures. They are not spoken to, they are spoken of:

20. And if ye wish to exchange one wife for another and ye have given unto one of them a sum of money (however great), take nothing from it. Would ye take it by the way of calumny and open wrong?

(Surah IV, "Women," p. 101)

49. O ye who believe! If ye wed believing women and divorce them before ye have touched them, then there is no period that ye should reckon. But content them and release them handsomely.

(Surah XXXIII, "The Clans," p. 556)

In this mode the linguistic schema that reflects the power schema is the following:

God ⟍

(speaks directly or indirectly through his prophet)

(to believing men) ↓

(believing women: believing men apply to them the

laws which they have received from the divine being)

The divine being addresses the one who has power over women in these instances — man. In this mode men and women do not have a symmetrical relationship with the divine being; they overlap each other in a pyramid that organizes and hierarchizes beings according to their relationship to power. The discourse, which is power, reflects in its very texture this pyramidal structure.

Symmetry between men and women in the elements of the divine discourse arranged according to the pyramidal schema would constitute an undermining of the pyramid; it would mean disorder and chaos. Thus, if you take Verse 20 of Surah IV and reverse the gender marking of the key words, you have a preposterous result: "If ye wish to exchange one wife for another" would become "If ye wish to exchange one husband for another."

This second phrase structures a preposterous world, because it leads us to imagine an order symmetrically opposite to the Muslim order, one where women would have the monopoly on the acts of marrying and repudiating their husbands. In the Muslim order only men can conclude an act of marriage (the woman is represented by a wali), and only men can have the privilege of repudiation.

## SACRED TIME AS A DEVICE
## FOR DISCRIMINATION: CHRONOLOGY AND BIOLOGY

In biological time, woman gives birth to man. It is the opposite in the realm of the sacred; woman is born after man and taken out of him; God first created men, and then he created women, whom he took out of them:

> 20. And of His signs is this: He created you of dust, behold you human beings, ranging widely!
> 21. And of His signs is this: He created for you helpmeets from yourselves that ye might find rest in them, and He ordained between you love and mercy. Lo! herein indeed are portents for folk who reflect.
>
> (Surah XXX, "The Romans," p. 532)

Sacred time turns biological time upside down and reconstructs the world according to antithetical data. The one who does not give birth, man, becomes the one who is given the power to engender. The one who gives birth, woman, not only sees her procreative capacity confiscated, but also becomes by a symmetrical reversal the one who is given birth to. The distribution of events in time — that is, chronology — determines at the same time the distribution of the power that beings have vis-à-vis each other. God first created men, and then he created women for them. He gave them wives taken out of them. In sacred time, the one who comes first possesses the one who comes after. The relationship between men and women is a relationship in which one element was created for the other, given to the other; this is a relationship of possession.

Time is one of the foundations of power; it is the first, and space comes afterward. The relationship of beings to power is closely wed to their relationship to time. Chronology determines the degree of power. The being who existed first is the divine being, and in him is concentrated all power and influence without restriction. All the beings who chronologically come after him have with him a relationship of dispossession as total and complete as their submission to him. Thus time is the very foundation of power, and it is manifested, incarnated, and actualized in a relationship of possession, whether with regard to space or to the beings who live in it.

God existed first, and then he created the world (relationship to space). God existed first, and then he created the angels, and after that, human beings (relationship to beings). This chronology inevitably creates a relationship of possession as regards space. The one who exists first, God, possesses what comes into existence afterward: the world and a hierarchical relationship to beings. (God is superior to all those who exist after him. The angels are inferior to God, but superior to human beings.)

It is the divine being who created nature, a space with which he maintains a precise hierarchical relationship. It is a relationship of possession, the most extreme of the hierarchical relationships, in which the partner possessed is deprived of will. In the relationship of possession there is no interchange; there are not two elements endowed with will. There is one element endowed with will and another without it.

In the divine being's design, human beings are not homogeneous entities who occupy an identical position and fulfill interchangeable duties vis-à-vis him. The schema that links the divine being to human beings is not a symmetrical relationship. That would imply equality between human beings whatever their sex or age.

In a scenario of symmetrical relationships, the three categories of human beings (men, women, and children) would all be equal. They would have an identical relationship with God:

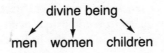

But in the sacred construction of reality the relationship that links the divine being to human beings is not symmetrical. Far from occupying interchangeable positions vis-à-vis him, human beings, carefully divided into distinct age and sex categories, are inserted into a pyramidal structure that hierarchizes them and subjects some to others. The pyramidal schema that orders the relationships between these distinct categories is not a marginal model. It is a central device for the application of sacred power. It is the mirror, the echo, and the logical extension of the universe as fashioned by the divine will.

In a scenario of pyramidal relationships, human beings are ranked by age and sex according to a discriminatory pyramid:

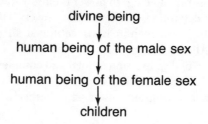

The schema of pyramidal relationships not only embodies a hierarchization of duties characterized by an increasing distance from the divine being and a multiplication of intermediaries. It also reflects the time sequence of creation. The male human being was created first, then the woman who came out of him, and finally the children who came out of her.

And here we come upon a fundamental distinction in the realm of the profane, the distinction between human beings and things, which becomes blurred when one moves to the realm of the sacred. Certain beings, women and children, classified as humans in the realm of the profane, are classified in the sacred realm as "lawful things" to be enjoyed by the male believer. The fact that the humanity of woman and child seems to be an intermittent given and not a constant reflects the subordinate place they occupy in the universal hierarchy. There is thus a convergence between chronology, the allotment of positions vis-à-vis the divine being, and finally the function of beings, for which the system has created them.

Each category of human beings was created according to a divine time sequence, deliberately and minutely calculated. This spacing in time expresses and actualizes a ranking in functions and purposes. If the adult human being of the male sex was created to serve God, women and children were created to serve, not God directly, but the adult male human being; only through him do they serve God. It is by fulfilling their function in attendance on the adult human being of the male sex that children serve God, who thus has an indirect and mediated relationship with them. The divine being, as the source and incarnation of power, delegates it to those who are charged with direct duties to him. Those who do not have that direct relationship have no power. Human beings deprived of power are ranked with material objects, with which they share their powerlessness. In more than one verse of the Koran, women and children are associated with the material riches that the divine being created for the gratification of the adult believer of the male sex:

14. Beautified for mankind is love of the joys (that come) from women and offspring, and stored-up heaps of gold and silver, and horses branded (with their mark), and cattle and land. That is comfort of the life of the world. Allah! With Him is a more excellent abode.
(Surah III, "The Family of 'Imran," pp. 63–64)

72. And Allah hath given you wives of your own kind, and hath given you, from your wives, sons and grandsons, and hath made provision of good things for you. . . .
(Surah XVI, "The Bee," p. 354)

46. Wealth and children are an ornament of the life of the world. . . .
(Surah XVIII, "The Cave," p. 386)

37. And it is not your wealth nor your children that will bring you near unto Us. . . .
(Surah XXIV, "Saba," p. 567)

In the sacred programming of creation,[5] food and union with women are among the lawful good things that the creator destined for the male believer:

5. This day are (all) good things made lawful for you. The food of those who have received the Scripture is lawful for you, and your food is lawful for them. And so are the virtuous women of the believers and the virtuous women of those who received the Scripture before you (lawful for you) when ye give them their marriage portions and live with them in honour, not in fornication, nor taking them as secret concubines. . . .
(Surah V, "The Table Spread," p. 135)

It is around these two pleasures — the pleasure of eating and the pleasure of union with women and having children — that the universe is organized. By examining the first of these pleasures, eating, we will see the structures of the economic politics of Islam emerge (Chapter 11), and by examining the second, the pleasure of union with women and having children, we will see the structures of the sexual politics of Islam emerge (Chapter 12). But before launching into these investigations, we must define sacred space and the beings who people it.

## SACRED SPACE AS DESIGN FOR DISCRIMINATION

Sacred space contains the earth, but is not limited to it. The beings who inhabit it include human beings and earthly animals, but are not limited to them. We need to identify sacred spaces and sacred beings in order to isolate the aspect that interests us — the schema of relationships between all these elements.

### Sacred Space: Duality and Inequality as the Relational Schema

The ecological field, where the sacred manifests itself, answers to a very precise ordering of time and space. These latter are first of all entities that are finite, limited, explored, recognized, programmed, and controlled. These two entities are then combined to create an ecological universe that is irreparably split into two distinct spaces, broken apart but linked into a fatal relationship of inequality, hierarchization, and domination — the earthly world and the Hereafter, Paradise. The dual existence of these two universes inevitably implies the relational schema that I have called inversion-linkage. The fall of one of the elements is brought on by the mere existence of the other; earthly life is devalued as a result of the existence of Paradise. The relationship between these two universes is programmed, fixed, and eternal; inequality as the equilibrium of the system and the code of its functioning is the law and the very manifestation of divine power. All activity that takes place in sacred "reality" only has meaning in relationship to that hierarchized ecological theater where, once again, the concrete, the material (earthly life) is evaluated as a "fall" compared with the invisible, the abstract, the imaginary (Paradise). Sacred time functions within rather narrow limits. Time is conceptualized in terms of three sequences: the beginning, the unfolding, the end. The beginning of an event has a determining effect, because it situates the event within the global system at the outset.

The appearance of earthly life is an event that comes after the existence of the Beyond, just as woman was created after man. The appearance of earthly life was in fact due to an accident; it should never have existed. In the original design, Adam and his wife were in Paradise. It was an unfortunate incident, an act of disobedience, a contravention of the law, which led to the appearance of the earth. And it was a punishment for Adam, a "fall":

> 19. O Adam! Dwell thou and thy wife in the Garden and eat from whence ye will, but come not nigh this tree lest ye become wrong-doers.
> 20. Then Satan whispered to them that he might manifest unto them that which was hidden from them of their shame, and he said: Your Lord forbade you from this tree only lest ye should become angels or become of the immortals.
> 22. Thus did he lead them on with guile. And when they tasted of the tree their shame was manifest to them and they began to hide (by heaping) on themselves some of the leaves of the Garden. And their Lord called them (saying): Did I not forbid you from that tree and tell you: Lo! Satan is an open enemy to you?
> 24. He said: Go down (from hence), one of you a foe unto the other. There will be for you on earth a habitation and provision for a while.
>
> (Surah VII, "The Heights," pp. 194–95)[2]

Earthly life is the mirrored inverse of Paradise. Every element valued positively in the one is valued negatively in the other. The pleasures of the earth are valued negatively because they are a potential distraction to the believer from the conduct imposed on him by the divine program. Earthly time is ephemeral. Compared to the eternity of Paradise, it loses all value. The quality of life on earth is mere play, amusement (*la'ib wa lahuw*), compared to the great "happy ending" that is life in Paradise:

> 20. Know that the life of the world is only play, and idle talk, and pageantry, and boasting among you, and rivalry in respect of wealth and children. . . .
>
> (Surah LVII, "Iron," p. 721)

Life on earth, the realm where human beings create and are re-created, is devalued and made subordinate to an imaginary space, Paradise, which by its mere existence dictates the fall of everything that is earthly. Inversion-linkage polarizes the opposing elements in a hierarchized and conflictual relationship and condemns the productive forces (concrete nature) to dispossession and sterility in their confrontation with the abstract, the imaginary (Paradise). In the sacred construction of reality, the structural code reverses the signs and values. It labels as inferior the agents and processes that produce material and human wealth and divests them of the power to create, which becomes the monopoly of the nonconcrete, the imaginary, of God and Paradise. The space that is the creator of riches is not only dispossessed but assigned its value by reference to the space that has confiscated its creativity — the imaginary.

The relationship of domination accompanies and is the logical and simultaneous result of the relationship of dispossession, and in this relationship the abstract, the imaginary is always the winner. The conflictual relationship between the material and the imaginary polarizes the energies of the sacred universe and diverts them from the great struggle to become human that the human being wages with nature. The same schema of relationships is found in the sacred population. The latter is composed of concrete beings and imaginary beings, and all are linked in a value scale that places some concrete beings in a position inferior to that of other concrete beings.

## The Sacred Population:
## The Angels as an Instrument for Downgrading Human Beings

The schema of relationships between beings (whether between the divine being and the human, between the angel and the human, between the divine and the angel, between the angel and the djinn, or between two human beings, especially man and woman) can only be understood in its overall context, by regarding the population as a whole as it exists in sacred time and space.

In the Muslim universe there are various categories of beings. Some have a concrete existence, others have an abstract one. The concrete beings are human beings and animals. They are visible, palpable, tangible. A human or animal being can be seen, heard, touched, and occasionally smelled or tasted. Besides this category of concrete beings, there is a category of abstract beings whose existence cannot be apprehended by the five senses. If it is decided to classify everything that is not concrete as imaginary, these are purely fictive beings. They are the divine being and another category distinct from the divine, which groups together beings as diversified as the angels and the djinns. These two categories of beings are linked by strictly codified relationships, whether within each category or outside it. The code is the inversion-linkage that we already found existing in space. God and the angels are superior to human beings. This is the reason why Satan refused to bow down before Adam:

> 12. He said: What hindered thee that thou didst not fall prostrate when I bade thee? (Iblis) said: I am better than him. Thou createdst me of fire while him Thou didst create of mud.
>
> (Surah VII, "The Heights," p. 192)

From the very beginning the imaginary and the concrete had a precise chronological relationship as regards beings: The imaginary (God and the angels) existed first, and it was God who then created the concrete (the human being). It was the divine being, God, who existed first, and he created all the other beings as well as the environment in which they live. The existence of God as the first event in the creation of the universe has a determining effect on the whole schema of relationships.

So we have seen that the sacred ecological field (sacred time, space, and population) is a universe with two components, the concrete and the abstract, and these two components are linked in a hierarchical relationship in which the concrete is always inferior to the abstract and judged by reference to it. The divine discourse creates a specific time where the sequence of events is different from the sequence of events in the concrete world.

In the divine discourse the angels existed before human beings, and among the latter men were born first, women afterward. This sacred chronology mirrors the conceptual structure of the unequal relationship that exists between angels and humans and between men and women.

With regard to space, Paradise is superior to the earth, and the latter is valued by reference to it. So sacred time and space encompass abstract spaces and beings along with concrete space and beings. And time and space are organized according to a schema of unequal relationships, which they put into effect and through which they manifest themselves.

Now that the theater of the universe has been delineated and space and its population described, we must look at the schema that regulates the relationship of the sacred population to the environment — that is, to natural resources. How does that population subsist and reproduce itself? How do these beings mobilize the resources that they need for survival? Is it by work or by some other process? It is obvious that our interest still lies in discovering if the relations between the sexes are exceptional or if they actualize and reproduce the fundamental schema of the Muslim order. In order to discover how woman subsists and under what conditions she has access to earthly nourishment, we must first find out under what conditions man himself subsists.

# 11 The Economic Field: The Link Between Worship and Consumption

We know that in legal Islam it is man who provides for woman. For example, the Moroccan Family Law,[1] promulgated in 1957, which has its source in *Al-Muwatta* of Malik Ibn Anas, states in Article 15: "Every person provides for his needs through his own resources, with the exception of the wife whose upkeep [*nafaqa*] is incumbent on her husband."[2]

Is the providing of *nafaqa*, the explicit economic relationship that is the foundation of the relationship between the sexes and the pillar of the Muslim family, a relationship unique of its kind and not found in other spheres, or is it simply the reflection of a structural schema that organizes all relationships in the economic field? Verse 34 of Surah IV of the Koran teaches us that the superiority of men over women is justified by the fact that men provide women with *nafaqa*, the resources necessary to maintain human life. Is the link between the relationship of domination and consumption limited to the sexual relationship, or is it institutionalized in other spheres?

How do men, women, and children subsist in the Muslim order? Is access to riches, to subsistence unconditional and unorganized, or does it follow a strict and precisely established code? The answer is that the quest for life in orthodox Islam follows a precise code in which each element and being occupies a defined place in the process of the creation and distribution of wealth. Nothing is left to chance; everything is codified and organized around a desire that is the end purpose of the universe and its reason for existence: God's desire to be worshipped.

The universe is organized, managed, and animated as the response to and incarnation of the divine will. The divine will is clear and not in the least ambiguous: It is God's desire to be worshipped at all times, eternally, and without interruption by the creatures that he created, in particular by the believer. This desire of God's to be worshipped without reserve or restraint, constantly, and eternally, is set forth and legitimated by and through a precise economic infrastructure: the fact that God possesses everything, material goods (riches, the environment, heaven and earth, and everything in between) and immaterial goods (knowledge, science, learning, the power of decision), and the fact that the believer possesses nothing — any goods that he might possess come to him from God.

It is not possible for the believer to acquire material or immaterial wealth except through the intermediary of the divine will. Wealth, food, shelter, and opulence are not achieved through human work. In the Muslim universe human work is not the creator of wealth. One acquires wealth by submission to him who possesses that wealth: God. Access to wealth and opulence is assured through allegiance to the possessor, the provider, the almighty, the proprietor.

The divine will is precisely this desire to reduce the will of the one who possesses nothing (the believer) to the will of the one who possesses everything (God). The dispossessed, the believer, dedicates his life to worshipping the provider, God; he must try to live every moment according to God's will and desires. There would be no problem if God's desire and men's spontaneous desires coincided. However, they apparently do not inevitably and spontaneously coincide.

God's desire to be worshipped by his servants, the believers, should not in the normal course of events pose any problem, for among God's qualities and attributes is omnipotence: It is enough for him to say something for it to be. Nevertheless, the worship that the master demands from the servant does not seem to be a spontaneous thing, and the whole Koran can be read as an attempt to eliminate the obstacles that threaten to thwart it. The entire holy book is a recognition that the master-servant relationship is far from being easily achievable. The worship of one being by another seems problematic even when the master is an omnipotent being who possesses the universe and controls it at will. Even for a God, making oneself worshipped seems to be a far from easy thing. The divine desire to be worshipped seems to run into certain obstacles that interfere in the relationship with the one he desires as his servant. These obstacles come essentially from the resistance that the servant's will and desires are bound to pose to the idea of worship. It seems that there is no inevitable coincidence between the wills and desires of two beings who enter into a hierarchical and unequal relationship, even when one of them is a God and the other a mere mortal.

The resistance that threatens to wreck the scheme for submission of one being to another comes from the slave, the inferior, the believer. So the obstacle to worship does not lie with the master but with the slave. It is the will and desires of the slave that threaten to ruin the scheme for the relationship of worship that the slave is supposed to dedicate to the master and not the reverse. The danger comes from below, not from above, from the weak party instead of the powerful one. The center of resistance to the scheme of submission by the believer to God is the will and desire of the believer, which threaten to come into conflict with those of God.

In this sense, the holy book of Islam is an attempt by the powerful party, God, to help the weak party, the believer, conquer the resistance that his will and desires threaten to pose to the scheme for submission. What are these threats? How can the believer curtail and master them?

The holy book is a system of laws that precisely answers this problem. The Koran is a treatise on the question of submission to the almighty and how to achieve it. It is a discourse that organizes the cosmic environment and the existence of the beings who people it in order to solve this problem, as it is viewed by the party that has the power and desires the submission of the other.

The universe in the discourse of orthodox Islam is a universe as viewed and desired by the almighty. Nowhere in the holy book do we have direct access to the point of view of the weak one, the servant, the slave, the believer whose submission God demands. We only have access to the servant through the master.

This fact is fundamental for viewing the relationship between the sexes as it is shaped by Muslim civilization. The relationship between the sexes is nothing but a reflection and incarnation of the fundamental relationship between God, the Master, and his slave, the believer. One of the givens of the relationship between the sexes, as Islam has designed and effected it, is that this relationship is shaped according to the desire of the master, the husband. The woman's desire is never directly expressed. It is unheard except when expressed through the mediation of the master. The political economy of Islam is set up and orchestrated around the silence of inferiors. This silence is the expression of the abolition of their will and the manifestation of their submission.

## THE POLITICAL ECONOMY OF ISLAM:
## WEALTH IN EXCHANGE FOR SUBMISSION

In analyzing all relationships in general and those called love relationships in particular, one must try to answer several questions: Who is speaking? Whose ideas are being expressed in the relationship? What is exchanged in the relationship, and who fixes the terms of the exchange? An egalitarian relationship would be one in which the two parties express themselves equally and give their points of view regarding the terms of exchange, the needs of each one, and how to satisfy them — in short, negotiate the terms of the exchange. On the contrary, an unequal relationship would be one in which one partner alone expresses his desires concerning the relationship and fixes the terms of exchange solely according to his own needs.

The relationship between the divine being and the believer is an example of the unequal type. The discourse on the relationship between the divine and the human is a monologue by the divine being. (For this part of the analysis the sole reference will be the Koran, which is the divine discourse and the key discourse for orthodoxy.) The Koran is the point of view of the divine being on the relationship that must exist between him and the human being. The Koran is the universe according to the desires and will of the divine being. Nowhere in the holy book are the desires and needs of the human being expressed directly. One only has access to them through the divine discourse, which alone constructs reality for the two parties. The sacred construction of reality is the expression and reflection of the desire and will of the almighty, and this desire and will are invested in one sole objective, which is the raison d'être of the universe itself — God's desire to be worshipped:

25. And We sent no messenger before thee but we inspired him, (saying): There is no God save Me (Allah), so worship me.

(Surah XXI, "The Prophets," p. 421)

56. O my bondmen who believe! Lo! My earth is spacious. Therefor serve Me only.

(Surah XXIX, "The Spider," p. 527)

36. And serve Allah. . . .

(Surah IV, "Women," p. 107)

The divine being's desire regarding the relationship that he would like to establish with the human being is expressed in the form of an order: "Worship me." This order is the expression of a power relationship that is legitimated by what God gives the believer in exchange. An egalitarian relationship presupposes reciprocity, that the goods and services furnished by one party have a value more or less similar to what is received in exchange. An egalitarian relationship presupposes an equal division of wealth from the start. It implies that the elements of exchange are of equal importance to the reciprocal needs of the two parties. An egalitarian relationship implies that the value of the elements pledged in the exchange is identical or at least equivalent. An exchange in which reciprocity is absent, in which the elements received do not have the same order of urgency and importance as the elements given, is an unequal exchange. And divine love seems to belong to this category.

The divine being and the human being have radically different relationships to the available wealth. One party, the divine being, has a monopoly of the wealth, and the other, the human being, is totally deprived of it:

6. Unto Him belongeth whatsoever is in the heavens and whatsoever is in the earth, and whatsoever is between them, and whatsoever is beneath the sod.

(Surah XX, "Ta Ha," p. 405)

The divine monopoly of everything that exists introduces an element that renders any idea of exchange in the relationship impossible. As a matter of fact, one of the parties, the human being, figures among the possessions of the other. The divine being owns the believer. The relationship of possession wipes out the possibility of exchange. In order for there to be exchange, there must be two wills that confront each other at the start and negotiate a relationship and fix its terms. So, in the sacred universe, which is a coherent and logical universe par excellence, the being possessed has no will:

23. And say not of anything: Lo! I shall do that tomorrow,
24. Except if Allah will. . . .

(Surah XVIII, "The Cave," p. 382)

In contrast to the absence of will in the human being, we find the omnipotence of the divine being. This divine power is embodied in the complete control of time and space and manifests itself in a minutely detailed and total programming of the least movement that animates beings and objects in the universe:

> 49. Lo! We have created every thing by measure.
> 52. And every thing they did is in the scriptures.
> 53. And every small and great thing is recorded.
>
> (Surah LIV, "The Moon," p. 707)

> 23. Thus We arranged. How excellent is Our arranging!
>
> (Surah LXXVII, "The Emissaries, p. 784)

Human beings have no control over the environment in which they live, nor their own existence. They live totally alienated in an ecological milieu where a will foreign to their own programs the smallest occurrence with ease:

> 22. Naught of disaster befalleth in the earth or in yourselves but it is in a Book before We bring it into being — Lo! that is easy for Allah —
>
> (Surah LVII, "Iron," p. 721)

Time is a divine monopoly. The essence of power, planning, programming, and action, time is completely out of the control of human beings, and they are thereby defined as being stripped of the capacity to make their own history, to have an impact on their own environment:

> 11. . . .And no one groweth old who groweth old, nor is aught lessened of his life, but it is recorded in a Book. Lo! that is easy for Allah.
>
> (Surah XXXV, "The Angels," p. 572)

> 34. And every nation hath its term, and when its term cometh, they cannot put it off an hour nor yet advance (it).
>
> (Surah VII, "The Heights," p. 196)

Not only do human beings not control time, but they themselves are programmed within a tight web of constant surveillance of their least actions:

> 29. . . .We have caused (all) that ye did to be recorded.
>
> (Surah XLV, "Crouching," p. 663)

> 16. We verily created man and We know what his soul whispereth to him, and We are nearer to him than his jugular vein.
> 17. When the two Receivers receive (him), seated on the right hand and on the left,
> 18. He uttereth no word but there is with him an observer ready.
>
> (Surah L, "Qaf," p. 688)

Not only do human beings not control time, but time itself in the sacred construction of reality, is metamorphosed into a prison, a trap. Sacred time is the surveillance of, and consequently the programmed frustration of, the slightest inclination toward self-determination by humans; the divine being watches and controls the least movement:

> 4. He is with you wheresoever ye may be. And Allah is Seer of what ye do.
> 6. He is Knower of all that is in the breasts.
>
> (Surah LVII, "Iron," p. 718)

And if time is surveillance, recording, control, and observation by a supreme authority, space also is answerable to the same authority and obedient to its will. Prisoners of time, humans are also prisoners in space, a space programmed, arranged, and connected to a will other than their own, that of divine power.

The human being's relationship to his environment is supplanted by the relationship between God and that environment. The human being only has access to the environment through the divine will. It is only because God created the world for the believer that this believer has access to it, and he is totally passive in this process. Everything has been arranged and organized according to a precisely elaborated divine plan:

> 12. And He hath constrained the night and the day and the sun and the moon to be of service unto you, and the stars are made subservient by His command. Lo! herein indeed are portents for people who have sense.
> 15. And He hath cast into the earth firm hills that it quake not with you, and streams and roads that ye may find a way.
>
> (Surah XVI, "The Bee," pp. 345–46)

> 6. Have We not made the earth an expanse,
> 7. And the high hills bulwarks?
> 8. And We have created you in pairs,
> 9. And have appointed your sleep for repose,
> 10. And have appointed the night as a cloak,
> 11. And have appointed the day for livelihood.
> 12. And We have built above you seven strong (heavens),
> 13. And have appointed a dazzling lamp,
> 14. And have sent down from the rainy clouds abundant water,
> 15. Thereby to produce grain and plant,
> 16. And gardens of thick foliage.
>
> (Surah LXXVIII, "The Tidings," p. 786)

In the sacred environment structured in this way, we now need to identify the modalities of men's access to the earth's riches. How can a man subsist? Are the available riches on earth immediately consumable, or do they require an intermediary process of transformation — namely, work?

## THE RELATIONS OF PRODUCTION
## IN THE SACRED ECONOMY: INEQUALTIY
## AS THE MODE OF ACCESS TO EARTHLY RICHES

The question to be examined first of all is the state of these riches: Are they raw, or are they in a state to be consumed? Answering this question permits us to clarify the status of one very important element of civilization, work. Is it necessary to work in order to subsist and survive, or does the survival of a human being depend on something else, and is it conditioned by other processes? The first answer is that no animal, no human being can assure its own subsistence:

60. And how many an animal there is that beareth not its own provision! Allah provideth for it and for you. He is the Hearer, the Knower.

(Surah XXIX, "The Spider," p. 528)

10. And We have given you (mankind) power in the earth, and appointed for you therein livelihoods. Little give ye thanks!

(Surah VII, "The Heights," p. 192)

64. Allah it is Who . . . fashioned you and perfected your shapes, and hath provided you with good things. . . .

(Surah XL, "The Believer, p. 625)

1. Lo! We have given thee Abundance;
2. So pray unto thy Lord, and sacrifice.

(Surah CVIII, "Abundance," p. 823)

It is clear that the means for survival, "good things" and "abundance," are immediately available, and it is God who has decreed it thus.

In the sacred economy, God created goods that are immediately utilizable by the human being. God created "warm clothing" and "riding" animals; he sends down "drinking" water from the sky; "causeth crops to grow . . . and the olive and the date-palm and grapes and all kinds of fruit." He put "fresh meat" in the sea:

5. And the cattle hath He created, whence ye have warm clothing and uses, and whereof ye eat;
6. And wherein is beauty for you, when ye bring them home, and when ye take them out to pasture.
7. And they bear your loads for you unto a land ye could not reach save with great trouble to yourselves. Lo! your Lord is Full of Pity, Merciful.
8. And horses and mules and asses (hath He created) that ye may ride them, and for ornament. And He createth that which ye know not.
10. He it is Who sendeth down water from the sky, whence ye have drink, and whence are trees on which ye send your beasts to pasture.

11. Therewith He causeth crops to grow for you, and the olive and the date-palm and grapes and all kinds of fruit. Lo! herein is indeed a portent for people who reflect.

12. And He hath constrained the night and the day and the sun and the moon to be of service unto you, and the stars made subservient by His command. Lo! herein indeed are the portents for people who have sense.

13. And whatsoever He hath created for you in the earth of divers hues, lo! therein is indeed a portent for people who take heed.

14. And He it is Who hath constrained the sea to be of service that ye eat fresh meat from thence, and bring forth from thence ornaments which ye wear. And thou seest the ships ploughing it that ye (mankind) may seek of His bounty, and that haply ye may give thanks.

(Surah XVI, "The Bee," pp. 344–46)

So here we have an economy of gatherers rather than one where the production of usable products entails an effort, specifically, work. This makes it interesting to discover how these riches are distributed, since no effort is required to make them consumable. Are they accessible to everyone? It seems that they are not. The distribution of riches is totally at the discretion of God, which in fact means his whim:

12. His are the keys of the heavens and the earth. He enlargeth providence for whom He will and straiteneth (it for whom He will). Lo! He is Knower of all things.

(Surah XLII, "Counsel," p. 638)

30. Lo! thy Lord enlargeth the provision for whom He will, and straiteneth it (for whom he will). . . .

(Surah XVII, "The Al-Isra," p. 367)

But the divine whim itself follows a precise plan — the creation of inequality among men:

32. . . . We have apportioned among them their livelihood in the life of the world, and raised some of them above others in rank that some of them may take labour from others. . . .

(Surah LXIII, "Ornaments of Gold," p. 649)

The plan for inequality among men does not stop at life on earth; it is prolonged and projected into the Hereafter also:

13. And every man's augury have We fastened to his own neck, and We shall bring forth for him on the Day of Resurrection a book which he will find wide open.

21. See how We prefer one of them above another, and verily the Hereafter will be greater in degrees and greater in preferment.

(Surah XVII, "The Al-Isra," pp. 365–66)

Not only is inequality among men a consequence of the divine will, but precisely because of this, it is blasphemy to upset it. Questioning the relationship of inequality is upsetting the divine design. A master who tries to become close to his slave, to divide his wealth with him in such a way as to give him more equality, is a being who violates divine will and upsets the divine plan:

71. And Allah hath favoured some of you above others in provision. Now those who are more favoured will by no means hand over their provision to those (slaves) whom their right hands possess, so that they may be equal with them in respect thereof. . . .

(Surah XVI, "The Bee," pp. 353–54)

This inequality is far from being a chance or an accident; it is the plan and the order; questioning it is disorder. The relationship of inequality represents the end purpose of the universe and is identical with the divine desire, that of being worshipped. The ideal believer is a man who bows down, who prostrates himself, is obedient and respectful of the will of the almighty, the will of him who possesses everything:

112. (Triumphant) are those who turn repentant (to Allah), those who serve (Him), those who praise (Him), those who fast, those who bow down, those who fall prostrate (in worship), those who enjoin the right and forbid the wrong and those who keep the limits (ordained) of Allah—And give glad tidings to believers!

(Surah IX, "Repentance," p. 260)

To obey the almighty, to fear the exalted one, to bow down and prostrate oneself are the behaviors that create success and acceptance:

51. . . . We hear and we obey. And such are the successful.
52. He who obeyeth Allah and His messenger, and feareth Allah, and keepeth duty (unto Him): such indeed are the victorious.

(Surah XXIV, "Light," p. 465)

29. . . . Thou (O Muhammad) seest them bowing and falling prostrate (in worship), seeking bounty from Allah and (His) acceptance. The mark of them is on their foreheads from the traces of prostration. . . .

(Surah XLVIII, "Victory," p. 682)

A successful man is a man whose body bears the mark of prostration, of submission, of bowing down to the exalted one. In fact, by bowing, kneeling, and prostrating himself, man is only following the universal pattern of behavior toward the possessor:

> 18. Hast thou not seen that unto Allah payeth adoration whosoever is in the heavens and whosoever is in the earth, and the sun, and the moon, and the stars, and the hills, and the trees, and the beasts, and many of mankind. . . .
> (Surah XXII, "The Pilgrimage," p. 434)

This unequal relationship is all the more total and complete because one of the parties, the superior, has no need of the inferior. God is sufficient unto himself. He does not need men; they can give him nothing: They are castrated of the power of reciprocity, the necessary basis for a relationship of equality:

> 38. Allah is the Rich, and ye are the poor.
> (Surah XLVII, "Muhammad," p. 676)

> 15. O mankind! Ye are the poor in your relation to Allah. And Allah! He is the Absolute, the Owner of Praise.
> (Surah XXXV, "The Angels," p. 573)

The nature of the exchange between the Master, God, and the servant, the believer, is detailed, specific, and allows for no ambiguity, because any ambiguity would risk a dangerous lack of comprehension, a faulty reading of the divine will. From the outset the two partners in the exchange have at their disposal entirely different assets to put into the balance, and it is this difference as to the substance to be exchanged that immediately introduces inequality and disequilibrium into the relationship. From the very start there is a difference in the needs as well as the assets that each of the partners can invest in the exchange. The need of God is a need of an affective order. He wants to receive worship and not material goods. By contrast, the needs of man, as they are defined by the divine, are needs of a material order, consumable wealth. The exchange is thus not only unequal because of the identity of the two parties — one being a powerful God possessing everything in the universe — but also because of the nature of the values exchanged: the material versus the affective. The poor one can only give the affective — worship. The rich one can only give what he has —material wealth.

In this sacred construction of the universe, one sees very clearly not only that inequality expresses the differences in identity and potentialities of the two parties, but also that it constitutes a division of work that is the result of the initial differences. The contribution of the strong, powerful one can only be economic. The offering of the weak, inferior, economically deprived one can only be affective. And given the overall context of the divine design, where we have seen that time and space express and effect an unequal relationship, the contribution of the weak one within the divine relationship is given a negative value. It is in no way a challenge to the superiority of the divine:

55. And warn [them], for warning profiteth believers.
56. I created the jinn and humankind only that they might worship Me.
57. I seek no livelihood from them, nor do I ask that they should feed Me.
58. Lo! Allah! He it is that giveth livelihood, Lord of unbreakable might.

(Surah LI, "The Winnowing Winds," p. 695)

One of the characteristics of the relationship of worship between God and man is its inflexibility. There are no other possible alternatives in the exchange as it is fixed by the almighty. Any alternative is an attack on the will and desire of the master. And man's love, as we have seen, is precisely his resignation to the will of another, his obliterating any thoughts of self-affirmation. For the weak one (here, man) worship means self-mutilation; it means cutting out the quality that is the mark of the human — the will and freedom to conceptualize alternatives, to upset the plans of others. For a human being, will means the possibility of questioning the design or plan of someone else. The worship that God demands of man requires him to excise from himself his capacity to formulate conceptions, create alternatives, produce changes, and question relationships and the system underlying them. Worship, which is an affective capacity, the impulse of love toward another, inevitably implies the paralysis of another capacity — that of will, of the exercise of liberty. Love, as the divine conceives, demands, and imposes it, is an exercise in self-mutilation and a design for the worshipper to kill in himself every day any impulses toward liberty, any impulses to change the status quo, the plan of the loved one. Any manifestation of the will of the lover, the worshipper, can only be a weakening of the loved one, God. The inversion-linkage, which we have seen in operation in other contexts, assumes here its most perfect form. Resignation to the will of another is not only the sole form of worship possible, but it can only continue to exist if the worshipper agrees to kill in himself every day any attempt or inclination to imagine alternatives, much less to put them into practice. For to do so would be to leave the terrain of love for the terrain of disputation, of new ideas — the forbidden terrain of *bid'a*!

In summary, one can say that the love relationship between man and God is a rigid and fixed plan in which the partners are linked in a static relationship where the unequal exchange only succeeds because the weaker party has agreed to excise his will, his freedom to imagine, to envisage, and eventually to assert alternatives. A being without will, freedom, or the capacity to imagine alternatives and elaborate systems different from the one under which he lives, has much more in common with a thing than a human, if the latter is defined as being the potentiality of change, the possibility of alternatives.

Before looking at how the love relationship between God and man is actualized in the domestic field in the man/woman relationship, we must explore, through Paradise as the ideal Muslim order, the ideal relational schema that organizes the paradisal society and how it differs from those established as model relationships on earth.

The interest in exploring the relationship schema in Paradise lies in the fact that it is an ideal, overall model. It gives us a plan for society in which God, beings, and the environment are organized according to the divine will, the whim of the almighty, without any possibility of will or freedom on the part of the weak one or any questioning of the status quo. For the difference between life on earth and life in Paradise is that in the latter the population is a select one, where only those who have achieved the total submission of their will to the almighty have been chosen. Demographically speaking, the difference between life on earth and Paradise is that the earthly population is heterogeneous. There are some men who have the possibility of carrying out the divine whim, submission. There are others who have the possibility of not conforming. The population of Paradise, on the contrary, is homogeneous.

So the paradisal model allows us to analyze better what happens in a third field, defined as problematic, the domestic field. For we will see that from the beginning women, the number one citizens in this field, are defined and identified for many reasons as problematic citizens. Their position in the divine plan is posed as a problem from the very start.

It is moreover very revealing to find that in the paradisal society the earthly woman is, if not replaced, at least given serious competition by a major rival: the houri. What messages does the Muslim order, in its vision of an ideal world, inscribe on the female body? If one regards Paradise and its organization, structure, and administration as the code of an ideal Muslim system, what does one find when one looks at the female body in Paradise — in Paradise viewed as a total context and coherent system?

Is the houri, the paradisal woman, the ideal, example, and model of femininity, different from the male body in Paradise, as a page on which to write messages? Does the houri, passivity in the extreme, signify only herself, or is she in fact the mirror image of male passivity?

Everything that exists and happens on earth has meaning only by reference to what happens in that twin space, Paradise, which is the standard, the ideal. It is for this reason that we have to understand the structure of Paradise, the organization of its space, the actors who confront each other there, and their means of survival. We need to find out how the two essential needs of the human being, food and reproduction, are taken care of in Paradise. What is the population of Paradise? Who are the beings who people it? What relationships do they have with each other and with the environment? How does this population survive, feed itself, and reproduce itself? Only the code that regulates life in Paradise can clarify what happens on earth.

# THE IDEAL ECONOMY:
# THE ECONOMIC STRUCTURE OF PARADISE,
# THE ECLIPSING OF THE WORK PROCESS

## The Mode of Production in Paradise: An Economy of Gatherers

Paradise is characterized by an abundance of riches, in sharp contrast with their scarcity on earth. These riches are available to the chosen, and they are not a cause of dispute among them. It is the access to Paradise that is problematic; once the chosen have succeeded in getting there, their needs are totally filled without any effort on their part.

The paradisal ecology is conceived as follows: The individual has but to stretch out his hand to be fed. Fruits and the flesh of fowls are ready to be gathered; beverages such as milk, honey, wine, and pure water flow in the rivers and shaded streams; the climate is mild; there is no need to adapt to rigors of weather.

The ecology of Paradise is an ecology where man and his milieu are in a state of perfect symbiosis and harmony. There is no conflict between the human being and his environment. The latter is perfectly adapted to the needs of the former. The daily routine of the believer in Paradise is reduced to a very limited range of activities: eating and reposing in the company of placid sexual partners, the houris. There is no work routine in Paradise. There is only a rest routine. Life is exempt from all struggle, Paradise being the absence of conflict and effort. Food (fruits, flesh of fowls) and drink (wine, milk, honey, water) are available in nature, on the trees, in the sky, in the rivers and streams. Metals and precious stones (gold, silver, pearls) and luxurious fabrics (silk, brocade) make up the daily wear of the citizen of Paradise. The furnishings in Paradise are reduced to couches, cushions, carpets, silver goblets, and so on:

> 12. And [Allah] hath awarded them for all that they endured, a Garden and silk attire;
> 13. Reclining therein upon couches, they will find there neither (heat of) a sun nor bitter cold.
> 14. The shade thereof is close upon them and the clustered fruits thereof bow down.
> 15. Goblets of silver are brought round for them, and beakers (as) of glass
> 16. (Bright as) glass but (made) of silver, which they (themselves) have measured to the measure (of their deeds).
> 17. There are they watered with a cup whereof the mixture is of Zanjabil,
> 18. (The water of) a spring therein, named Salsabil.
> 19. There wait on them immortal youths, whom, when thou sees, thou wouldst take for scattered pearls.[3]
>
> (Surah LXXVI, " 'Time' or 'Man'," p. 781)

Paradise is a space where only one human activity is operational: repose. There is a total absence of the idea of work, which implies conflict, the necessity of exertion, and an unbalanced relationship between man and his environment from the start.

Nevertheless, despite the absence of a necessity for work or exertion, despite the great generosity of nature, there are servants there. They are of the male sex, young, and their raison d'être is to serve the believer:

> 12. In gardens of delight;
> 13. A multitude of those of old
> 14. And a few of those of later time.
> 15. On lined couches,
> 16. Reclining therein face to face.
> 17. There wait on them immortal youths
> 18. With bowls and ewers and a cup from a pure spring
> 19. Wherefrom they get no aching of the head nor any madness,
> 20. And fruit that they prefer
> 21. And flesh of fowls that they desire.
> 22. And (there are) fair ones with wide, lovely eyes,
> 23. Like unto hidden pearls,
> 24. Reward for what they used to do.
> 25. There they hear no vain speaking nor recrimination
> 26. (Naught) but the saying: Peace, (and again) Peace.
> 27. And those on the right hand; what of those on the right hand?
> 28. Among thornless lote-trees
> 29. And clustered plantains,
> 30. And spreading shade,
> 31. And water gushing,
> 32. And fruit in plenty
> 33. Neither out of reach nor yet forbidden,
> 34. And raised couches;
> 35. Lo! We have created them a (new) creation
> 36. And made them virgins,
> 37. Lovers, friends,
> 38. For those on the right hand;
>
> (Surah LVI, "The Event," pp. 713–14)

Here we see appearing another citizen of the paradisal society, the houri. The houris are created by God. They are faultless, young, loving, and virginal. God has created them for "those on the right hand," those who have succeeded in passing the test of unconditional worship on earth — having killed within themselves any will capable of disturbing the order, of questioning the divine whim and the world as structured by that whim.

We will keep in mind, then, four characteristics of the paradisal economy:

1. The abundant, generous, and immediately consumable nature.
2. The short-circuiting of the work process, made unnecessary by the generosity of the environment, with gathering being the most complex act that the chosen have to perform.

3. Division of the male population of Paradise into two groups according to function, one of which is subjected to the other, the group of servants being assigned to serve the group of the chosen.
4. Certain ambiguities and incoherencies in this programmed, coherent, and rational world, with regard to the division of the population of Paradise by sex and the organization of the process of reproduction.

### The Paradisal Mode of Reproduction:
### Duel Between Sterile Houris and Phantom Earthly Women

Although the mode of economic production in Paradise is very clearly specified in the Koran, a book which defines the code of every element and mechanism and situates them in a total system characterized by an implacable logic and faultless coherence, it turns out that the paradisal mode of reproduction is an area where there are certain ambiguities. This is particulary the case in the relationship between the houri (the paradisal woman) and the earthly woman, and in the relationship of these two women with the believer. Another ambiguity is the existence and status of children in paradisal space.

## THE CONDITIONS OF CITIZENSHIP
## IN PARADISE: MALENESS AND MATURITY

What is the demographic and social composition of the population of Paradise? Do all the individuals who live there enjoy the same status, or are they linked to each other by hierarchized relationships? Does the family unit exist and is it operational? Does the paradisal family function on the concept of the couple? There is a contradiction (and they are rare in the Koran) between citizenship in Paradise according to allotting and equipping of space and citizenship in terms of access to Paradise. Although access to Paradise is guaranteed to earthly women, directly as believers and indirectly as wives of men believers, Paradise is equipped solely for the happiness of men. The presence of eternally young and beautiful sexual partners, the houris, seems to make the sojourn of earthly women there a matter of unhappiness and anxiety rather than of happiness and delight. Several verses identify earthly women as having rights as believers that would merit entry to Paradise on a footing of equality with men:

> 97. Whosoever doeth right, whether male or female, and is a believer, him verily We shall quicken with good life, and We shall pay them a recompense in proportion to the best of what they used to do.
>
> (Surah XVI, "The Bee," p. 358)

> 124. And whoso doeth good works, whether of male or female, and he (or she) is a believer, such will enter paradise and they will not be wronged the dint in a date-stone.
>
> (Surah IV, "Women," p. 122)

In other verses access to Paradise is guaranteed to earthly women as wives. In these verses wives clearly have the right to all the benefits enjoyed by men, including eternity:

> 70. Enter the Garden, ye and your wives, to be made glad.
> 71. Therein are brought round for them trays of gold and goblets, and therein is all that souls desire and find sweet. And ye are immortal therein.
> 72. And this is the Garden which ye are made to inherit because of what ye used to do.
>
> (Surah XLIII, "Ornaments of Gold," p. 653)

But when you look at the spatial logistics, how space is organized and equipped in Paradise, you realize that it is a space equipped, on the level of sexuality, solely for the believer of the male sex. Not only does he have a sexual partner, the houri, who makes the earthly wife's value to her husband extremely marginal, but also nowhere in Paradise are the needs of this earthly woman taken into consideration. There is, for example, an amazing indifference to woman's sexual needs in Paradise, in contrast to the great detail with which the man's orgasmic satisfaction is programmed. There are several descriptions of Paradise in the Koran, one as beautiful as the other, but the one in Surah LV, "The Beneficent," is surely the most brilliant and musical. The arrangement and variety of the pleasures described there assure total gratification to the believer of the male sex, who seems to be the only inhabitant who matters:

> 46. But for him who feareth the standing before his Lord there are two gardens.
> 47. Which is it, of the favours of your Lord, that ye deny?
> 48. Of spreading branches.
> 49. Which is it, of the favours of your Lord, that ye deny?
> 50. Wherein are two fountains flowing.
> 51. Which is it, of the favours of your Lord, that ye deny?
> 52. Wherein is every kind of fruit in pairs.
> 53. Which is it, of the favours of your Lord, that ye deny?
> 54. Reclining upon couches lined with silk brocade, fruit of both the gardens near to hand.
> 55. Which is it, of the favours of your Lord, that ye deny?
> 56. Wherein are those of modest gaze, whom neither man nor jinni will have touched before them.
> 57. Which is it, of the favours of your Lord, that ye deny?
> 58. (In beauty) like the jacynth and the coral-stone.
> 59. Which is it, of the favours of your Lord, that ye deny?
> 60. Is the reward of goodness aught save goodness?
> 61. Which is it, of the favours of your Lord, that ye deny?
> 62. And beside them are two other gardens.
> 63. Which is it, of the favours of your Lord, that ye deny?
> 64. Dark green with foliage.

65. Which is it, of the favours of your Lord, that ye deny?
66. Wherein are two abundant springs.
67. Which is it, of the favours of your Lord, that ye deny?
68. Wherein is fruit, the date-palm and pomegranate.
69. Which is it, of the favours of your Lord, that ye deny?
70. Wherein (are found) the good and beautiful —
71. Which is it, of the favours of your Lord, that ye deny? —
72. Fair ones, close-guarded in pavilions —
73. Which is it, of the favours of your Lord, that ye deny? —
74. Whom neither man nor jinni will have touched before them —
75. Which is it, of the favours of your Lord, that ye deny? —
76. Reclining on green cushions and fair carpets.
77. Which is it, of the favours of your Lord, that ye deny?
78. Blessed be the name of thy Lord, Mighty and Glorious!

(Surah LV, "The Beneficent," pp. 710–12)

Other verses give detailed information about the houris — their eyes, the state of their hymen, their age, their character — while nowhere in the text are found similar descriptions detailing, if not the beauty, at least the modest or even perhaps hidden assets of earthly wives. In these lengthy descriptions of Paradise, the houri seems to find her perfect place in an ideal, harmonious environment, which she overwhelms with her presence and beauty to the point where it becomes difficult to imagine the earthly wife there. In the light of such descriptions the earthly wife becomes more and more a phantom, if not a sour note in the divine harmony.

There are even verses that specify, without the least equivocation, that the status of houris in Paradise is that of wives. This places the rivalry between earthly woman and houri on a very precise terrain — the legitimacy of the relationship:

51. Lo! those who kept their duty will be in a place secure
52. Amid gardens and watersprings,
53. Attired in silk and silk embroidery, facing one another.
54. Even so (it will be). And We shall wed them unto fair ones with wide, lovely eyes.
55. They call therein for every fruit in safety,
56. They taste not death therein, save the first death. . . .⁴

(Surah XLIV, "Smoke," pp. 658–59)

The houri is explicitly designated as "wedded" to the believer. She is an integral part of the equipment of paradisal space, which is organized around the idea of repose. The presence of the earthly wife in paradisal space would create, at the very least, a disharmonious note, if not a discordant one. In any case, she constitutes a disturbance of the paradisal objective, the quiet life, insofar as her place is already occupied. Her role on earth, that of primary sexual partner, has already been allotted.

As we have seen, one of the characteristics of Islam as a blueprint for human life is its coherence and almost mathematical logic. Confusions, ambiguities, and incoherencies are foreign to the Muslim order. The status of the earthly wife and her role in Paradise represents one of those rare instances where the Muslim system allows the existence of a fuzzy area, a zone of doubt. Now we must draw some overall conclusions about the economic field in general and the paradisal economy in particular before dealing with the domestic field, where we will try to find the elements of an answer to the ambiguity that surrounds the status of the earthly woman in Paradise.

## THE FEMALE MODEL AS MIRROR
## OF THE MALE CONDITION: DECODING THE HOURI

Decoding Paradise, its citizens, and their raisons d'être means decoding the ideal Muslim order and elucidating its foundations and its conception of beings and their purpose. How is the houri to be understood? What paradisal value system does she represent? What differences and similarities are there between her condition and that of the male believer? Do they have the same or different functions? And what are the raisons d'être of the houri and the male believer in the sacred economic field in its overall context?

The houri is defined in physical terms. She has no spiritual dimension; she is a thing because she has neither will nor any possibility of development. She is created to be consumed as a sexual partner by the male believer. Her value comes from her physical beauty, which God gives as a gift to the believer. Her purpose is to be consumed as a body lacking any will or specific aim. She is stripped of the human dimension, if one defines human as the possibility of developing in various ways and thus partaking of the unexpected, the unplanned. A human being is distinguished from the other animals by the capacity to surprise, to choose one path of development among many possibilities, to be free and able to escape all strict and rigid programming.

The houri is not human because she is deprived of her freedom of choice, of development. She has been created for one sole destiny: to be consumed by the male believer in a solely fetishizing sexual relationship, a relationship between two automatons without intellectual or spiritual dimensions. The houri has no intellect; she does not think. She is a thing that awaits consumption. And as such, she is the mirror image of the male condition in Paradise.

The male believer is an automaton. He is a being reduced to a digestive tube and a genital apparatus—a genital apparatus, moreover, deprived of its creative function, for the houri is a virgin. The genitality of the believer is stripped of its capacity for giving life, for projecting itself into the future.

Paradise, with its food and its houri, is programmed for a consumer-believer deprived of the creative dimension. The believer is fulfilled in Paradise by renouncing all the potentialities that define a human being, all possibilities of making choices not programmed by an external will. The purpose of the believer is to fit himself into the plan organized, conceived, and programmed by another will. The purpose of the believer is to reduce himself to a consumer and annihilate within himself his creative potential, for to create within the paradisal context would be to disturb the order and destroy the plan. The believer is passive: He digests, makes love to a houri deprived of a uterus (for she is a virgin), and relaxes. Like the houri, he forms an integral part of a system where he exists as a thing deprived of will. The only difference is that the houri is consumed as an object by the believer, and he is consumed as an object by the system. In the Muslim Hereafter, where one would expect that the spiritual dimension of the being would be magnified, one witnesses the metamorphosis of the human being into a thing. In the ideal society of Islam, the ideal citizen, the successful believer, is an automaton reduced to a few limited, programmed movements of the digestive track and genital apparatus. His end is a state of passivity. Any attempt on his part to escape this passive state would be an attack on the paradisal equilibrium. The houri is the mirror and epitome of this passivity. It is her very passivity that the believer desires. The paradisal female model, far from being of minor importance, represents the actual principle that is the foundation of the Muslim Hereafter. And the principle of passivity, which is the keystone of the paradisal system, the Muslim ideal of society, is also the keystone of the domestic field as it is designed and programmed by Muslim family laws.

# 12 The Domestic Field: The Fetishization of Sexuality

In the sacred construction of reality, Islam identifies the domestic field as the space of sexuality. Sexuality is removed from other spaces and confined, localized, and established in the domestic field. Outside of this field, sexuality is illicit. Only domestic sexuality is licit, and domestic sexuality (as it is interpreted by the Muslim cultural order) is a sexuality castrated of the two components of human sexuality: desire and reproduction. If castration is "the operation by which an individual, male or female, is deprived of the capacity of self-reproduction" (*Petit Robert*), then the Muslim domestication of sexuality precisely institutionalizes the castration of the capacity to give birth and the capacity for desire. But this double castration is planned and actualized in different ways according to sex. While the castration of the capacity to give birth, although it sterilizes both man and woman, is carried out on the female body, the castration of the capacity for desire is carried out on the male body, as we will see below. In both cases, the mutilations suffered by the body of one of them have immediate and mutilating repercussions on the other.

It is in the process of castration that there emerges a phenomenon that the Muslim order tries to negate: the sameness of male and female. The whole Muslim order, as a construction of reality, is directed toward liquidating the identity, the similarity of female and male. Setting up differences between the two is one of the pillars of the hierarchy.

It is obvious that a man resembles a woman much more than he does a god. One could say that Muslim reality as an interpretation of the concrete world is a universal strategy for negating the existence of the human couple. In the two operations of castration that we are going to analyze, it is the couple that is negated in both instances; and the couple's most important manifestations, which are also the strongest links binding male and female (the capacity for desire and for giving birth), are meticulously excised and offered as a sacrifice to the invisible being without material existence — the divine.

## CASTRATION OF THE FEMALE BODY OF ITS CAPACITY FOR REPRODUCTION: THE NEGATIVE ATTITUDE OF ISLAM TOWARD THE CONJUGAL FAMILY

We have seen that the paradisal female ideal, the houri, is an eternally virgin woman, without a uterus. In Muslim reality, the earthly woman is also deprived of a uterus; she is incapable of giving life; it is God who gives life, not woman.

## Reproduction as the Foundation of the Divine Power
## to Program the Universe: The Negative Attitude of Islam toward Children

It is God who creates the human being; woman is only the passive receptacle:

49. Unto Allah belongeth the Sovereignty of the heavens and the earth. He createth what He will. He bestoweth female (offspring) upon whom He will, and bestoweth male (offspring) upon whom He will;

50. Or He mingleth them, males and females, and He maketh barren whom He will. Lo! He is Knower, Powerful.

(Surah XLII, "Counsel," p. 645)

11. Allah created you from dust, then from a little fluid, then He made you pairs (the male and female). No female beareth or bringeth forth save with His knowledge. . . .

(Surah XXXV, "The Angels," p. 572)

20. Did We not create you from a base fluid
21. Which We laid up in a safe abode
22. For a known term?
23. Thus We arranged. How excellent is Our arranging!

(Surah LXXVII, "The Emissaries," p. 784)

47. Unto Him is referred (all) knowledge of the Hour. And no fruits burst forth from their sheaths, and no female carrieth or bringeth forth but with His knowledge. . . .

(Surah XLI, "Fussilat," p. 635)

5. . . . And We cause what We will to remain in the wombs for an appointed time, and afterward We bring you forth as infants, then (give you growth) that ye attain your full strength. . . .

(Surah XXII, "The Pilgrimage," p. 432)

By robbing woman of the giving of life and reducing her to a mere passive envelope in the creation process, God is confronted with the problem of sexual duality: how to retrieve the couple and how to re-create it. It will be reconstituted, but after having undergone a metamorphosis that negates the attribute of femaleness, the capacity to give birth. In sacred reality, it is man who gives birth to woman. The couple is reconstituted, not by fecundation, that is, sexual reproduction, but by parthenogenesis, asexual reproduction. Woman comes out of man. There is scission, not union:

36. Thinketh man that he is to be left aimless?
37. Was he not a drop of fluid which gushed forth?
38. Then he became a clot; then (Allah) shaped and fashioned
39. And made of him a pair, the male and female.
40. Is not He (Who doeth so) Able to bring the dead to life?

(Surah LXXV, "The Rising of the Dead," p. 779)

In order for the Hereafter to exist, God must be able to give life to the dead. And that is only possible if he takes away the giving of life on earth from woman. She gives birth to mortal earthly beings who have no development other than physical. The child born from the coupling of a man and a woman cannot be resurrected after death. For the mortal child, born of male/female union, to become a citizen of the sacred universe — that is, to become immortal — it is necessary to liquidate sexual reproduction. It is necessary to castrate woman of her capacity to give birth.

The Muslim woman is a special female; her biology does not obey the laws of the material world. Sacred biology depends on other laws and other principles. It is an inverted biology, where old women give birth as well as virgins and barren women. Abraham's wife is an example of a woman giving birth in old age:

> 71. And his wife, standing by, laughed when We gave her good tidings (of the birth) of Isaac, and, after Isaac, of Jacob.
> 72. She said: Oh, woe is me! Shall I bear a child when I am an old woman, and this my husband is an old man? Lo! this is a strange thing!
> 73. They said: Wonderest thou at the commandment of Allah? The mercy of Allah and His blessings be upon you, O people of the house! Lo! He is Owner of Praise, Owner of Glory!
>
> (Surah XI, "Hud," p. 294)

In the example of Mary, it is a virgin woman who gives birth. Sexual union as the creator of life is eliminated:

> 16. And make mention of Mary in the Scripture, when she had withdrawn from her people to a chamber looking East,
> 17. And had chosen seclusion from them. Then we sent unto her Our Spirit and it assumed for her the likeness of a perfect man.
> 18. She said: Lo! I seek refuge in the Beneficent One from thee, if thou art God-fearing.
> 19. He said: I am only a messenger of thy Lord, that I may bestow on thee a faultless son.
> 20. She said: How can I have a son when no mortal hath touched me, neither have I been unchaste?
> 21. He said: So (it will be). Thy Lord saith: It is easy for Me. And (it will be) that We make of him a revelation for mankind and a mercy from Us, and it is a thing ordained.
> 22. And she conceived him, and she withdrew with him to a far place.
>
> (Surah XIX, "Mary," pp. 396–97)

The example of Zachariah gives us an instance in which a barren woman, married to an old and feeble man, will give birth by divine will:

2. A mention of the mercy of thy Lord unto His servant Zachariah.

3. When he cried unto his Lord a cry in secret,

4. Saying: My Lord! Lo! the bones of me wax feeble and my head is shining with grey hair, and I have never been unblest in my prayer to Thee, my Lord.

5. Lo! I fear my kinsfolk after me, since my wife is barren. Oh, give me from Thy presence a successor

6. Who shall inherit of me and inherit (also) of the house of Jacob. And make him, my Lord, acceptable (unto Thee).

7. (It was said unto him): O Zachariah! Lo! We bring thee tidings of a son whose name is John; We have given the same name to none before (him).

8. He said: My Lord! How can I have a son when my wife is barren and I have reached infirm old age?

9. He said: So (it will be). Thy Lord saith: It is easy for Me, even as I created thee before, when thou wast naught.

(Surah XIX, "Mary," pp. 395–96)

Thus sacred biology reverses the earthly order. The young woman who is of an age for procreation is barren, and the old woman is fertile. And when man and woman mate in the sacred order, it is not their union that is the creative event, but the divine will. In the sacred universe the child becomes a commodity in the divine strategy of reward and punishment. The child, like other earthly riches, is bestowed upon the believer or denied to him according to divine will:

3. Lo! it is thy insulter (and not thou) who is without posterity.

(Surah CVIII, "Abundance," p. 823)

Sacred fertility is not based on biology but on submission to the divine will. The believer who does not submit, who does not love God and his prophets, will be struck with sterility.

The divine will declares itself to be firmly against the institution of the biological family (the man/woman/child triad). The Muslim God is a god who rejects having consort and child, seeing it as a degrading situation that detracts from his glory:

3. And (we believe) that He—exalted be the glory of our Lord!—hath taken neither wife nor son,

4. And that the foolish one among us used to speak concerning Allah an atrocious lie.

(Surah LXXII, "The Jinn," p. 769)

101. The Originator of the heavens and the earth! How can He have a child, when there is for Him no consort, when He created all things, and is Aware of all things?

(Surah VI, "Cattle," p. 178)

And it is precisely because he neither begets nor is begotten that he is a superior being. Procreation circumscribes the being in a triple-sequence process: beginning, development, end — birth, life, death. The divine being in his temporal rhythm is infinite; he knows neither beginning nor end:

1. Say: He is Allah, the One!
2. Allah, the eternally Besought of all!
3. He begetteth not nor was begotten.
4. And there is none comparable unto Him.

(Surah CXII, "The Unity," p. 825)

The negative attitude of the Muslim order toward children is expressed in several ways. The first is with regard to the child's access to Paradise, which is subject to certain conditions. The child's status in Paradise, like that of woman, is somewhat ambiguous. We have already noted that the ideal woman, the houri, is eternally virgin, and therefore incapable of giving children to the believer. Although children are in principle admitted to Paradise, it seems that this access (according to Surah LII, "The Mount") is not automatic and is a matter of concern for fathers on earth. This access appears to be conditional upon the child having adopted the faith of the father, that is, the Muslim faith:

21. And they who believe and whose seed follow them in faith, We cause their seed to join them (there), and We deprive them of nought of their (life's) work. Every man is a pledge for that which he hath earned.
22. And We provide them with fruit and meat such as they desire.
23. There they pass from hand to hand a cup wherein is neither vanity nor cause of sin.
24. And there go round, waiting on them menservants of their own, as they were hidden pearls.
25. And some of them draw near unto others, questioning,
26. Saying: Lo! of old, when we were with our families, we were ever anxious;
27. But Allah hath been gracious unto us and hath preserved us from the torment of the breath of Fire.

(Surah LII, "The Mount," pp. 696-97)

The believer's anxiety about the fate of his family is justified, in that the sacred sees a danger in the family and is actually in conflict with it. In the sacred universe, kinship allegiance does not necessarily coincide with divine allegiance. The Koran gives several examples of families broken up because of conflict between these two allegiances. One of these is the case of Lot, who was obliged to abandon his wife:

32. . . . We are to deliver him and his household, all save his wife, who is of those who stay behind.

33. And when Our messengers came unto Lot, he was troubled upon their account, for he could not protect them; but they said: Fear not, nor grieve! Lo! we are to deliver thee and thy household, (all) save thy wife, who is of those who stay behind.

(Surah XXIX, "The Spider," p. 524)

Another example is that of Abraham, who was obliged to disown his father:

114. The prayer of Abraham for the forgiveness of his father was only because of a promise he had promised him, but when it had become clear unto him that he (his father) was an enemy to Allah he (Abraham) disowned him. . . .

(Surah IX, "Repentance," pp. 260–61)

Another example is that of Noah, who was forced to abandon his son:

45. And Noah cried unto his Lord and said: My Lord! Lo! my son is of my household! Surely Thy promise is the Truth and Thou art the Most Just of Judges.

46. He said: O Noah! Lo! he is not of thy household; lo! he is of evil conduct, so ask not of Me that whereof thou hast no knowledge. I admonish thee lest thou be among the ignorant.

(Surah XI, "Hud," p. 290)

The believers' anxiety about their families brings out one of the most bizarre characteristics of the sacred: a relentless and systematic hatred of the believer's family, especially a polarization of that hatred around the wife and children, identified as enemies of the system.

This animosity of the Muslim God toward the wife and child as a potential source of pleasure and thus of affective and emotional investment for the believer ultimately manifests itself in a phenomenon already mentioned: the reification of the wife and child and their reduction to the status of "wealth," deprived of will, just like horses, gold, or other material objects.

The distinction between material wealth and human wealth (human agents), significant in the profane approach to concrete matters, is totally absent in the realm of the sacred. The same code that governs access to and consumption of material goods governs access to and "consumption" of human resources as objects of emotional and sexual enjoyment. Economics and sexuality are indissociable in the sacred construction of reality.

For the sacred order to exist, the female element (along with the child as a manifestation of it) has to be liquidated, because it is the incarnation of the finite, the mortal.

It is interesting to note that parallel to the ideological liquidation of the female element in Islam as a new discourse, this element was at the same time eliminated from the historical world. The pre-Islamic Arab goddesses had to be destroyed to make possible the assertion in heaven and on earth of the domination of the male element — that is, monotheism or the reign of the abstract.

## The Historical Liquidation
## of the Female Element: The Destruction of the Arab Goddesses

When the prophet Muhammad, the messenger of Allah, began his mission, not only was the Arab heaven occupied by various male gods, but a considerable part of that heaven was controlled by goddesses. In Ibn al-Qalbi's work, *The Book of Idols*, which is one of the key documents on the pre-Islamic religions, the three goddesses, Al-Lat, Al-Uzza, and Al-Manat, are identified as having a special importance in the Arab pantheon of the seventh century.[1] Al-Uzza, according to him, "was the most important idol among the Quraysh. They performed pilgrimages to her, gave offerings to her, and sought reconciliation with her through sacrifices." According to Ibn al-Qalbi, she was respected by all the Arabs. Her cult extended throughout Arabia as far as Mesopotamia. Goddess of the Quraysh, the tribe from which the prophet of Islam was to appear, her cult enjoyed a privileged importance, precisely because of its link to the hegemony of the Quraysh in the fifth and sixth centuries and their control of the caravan routes. Her hold on the popular imagination is supposed to have been deep-seated:[2] "She was mother earth, the counterpart of Demeter, controlling fecundity and the phenomena of generation."[3]

Al-Uzza was not alone. She occupied a prominent place, but she was not the sole incarnation of female divinity. Two other goddesses, Al-Manat and Al-Lat, also enjoyed particular prominence: the first with the tribe of the Aws and Hazraj, and the second with the tribe of the Taqif.[4] Like Al-Uzza, their cults were not limited to one tribe, but were spread throughout all of Arabia.

The cult of the goddesses presented a thorny problem for the messenger of Allah. He would not be able to monopolize power and establish the bases of the monotheistic religion unless these three goddesses were not only discredited but destroyed. Goddesses of fecundity, of generation, of sexual reproduction, they had to be liquidated if Allah and Islam were to triumph. This liquidation was carried out in two ways: ideologically, through discourse; and concretely, through the physical destruction of the sanctuaries of these goddesses.

Ideologically, the attack against the three goddesses was to be carried out on the level of the word. The divine, as the power to baptize, to rewrite reality, and to give names to the world, to beings, and things, impugned the three Arab goddesses by reducing them to mere words without content:

> 19. Have ye thought upon Al-Lat and Al-'Uzza
> 20. And Manat, the third, the other?
> 21. Are yours the males and His the females?
> 22. That indeed were an unfair division!
> 23. They are but names which ye have named, ye and your fathers, for which
> Allah hath revealed no warrant. . . .
>
> (Surah LIII, "The Star," p. 700)

Al-Lat, Al-Manat, and Al-Uzza had to become names without power, for, from that time onward, the power of words would come from God, from Allah. In order for Allah to be able to monopolize the power of giving names to the universe, that is, creating it by and through discourse, he had to succeed in cutting the umbilical cord with the goddess — mother or daughter.[5] And the confusion in the minds of the Arabs, among whom Muhammad preached the new religion, came precisely from the fact that they did not understand very well how a god could appear from nowhere without being linked in some way or other to a woman in a relationship of "generation." In their minds the three goddesses became the daughters of Allah, and Allah was going to have a lot of difficulty getting rid of these offspring bestowed on him by the Arab tribes. The recalcitrant Arabs called the three goddesses "*Banat Allah*," daughters of Allah.[6] But God protested strongly against being given any such progeny:

39. Or hath He daughters whereas ye have sons?

(Surah LII, "The Mount," p. 698)

15. And they allot to Him a portion of His bondmen! Lo! man is verily a mere ingrate.
16. Or chooseth He daughters of that He hath created, and Honoureth He you with sons?

(Ssurah XLIII, "Ornaments of Gold," p. 647)

57. And they assign unto Allah daughters — Be He glorified! — and unto themselves what they desire;

(Surah XVI, "The Bee," p. 351)

The confusion was troubling and concerned a very crucial point for the existence of the divine, namely, the liquidation of the female element along with sexual reproduction. In addition to the verbal destruction of the goddesses, it was necessary to proceed to their physical destruction. Manat's sanctuary was destroyed in the year eight of the Hegira:

The Quraysh and all the Arabs continued to respect her. It went on like this until the prophet (may God's blessing and peace be with him) left Medina in the year eight of the Hegira, which was the year in which Allah assured him success. When he was four or five nights distant from Medina, he sent to her (Manat) Ali, who destroyed her and expropriated all she possessed.[7]

Al-Lat received the same treatment after the tribe of Ta'if became Muslim. Al-Mugira Ibn Su'ba destroyed and burned her sanctuary.[8] Al-Uzza suffered the same fate. According to Ibn al-Qalbi:

Al-Uzza continued in this way [that is, being worshipped] until Allah sent his prophet (may God's blessing and peace be with him). The latter discredited her, as well as the other idols, and counselled them [the people] to stop worshipping her. Finally, the Koran settled the question.[9]

Khalid Ibn al-Walid, to whom the prophet entrusted the mission of destroying her, had to make several attempts to carry it out.[10] He had to get up courage to confront the goddess in the form of "an Abyssinian woman with disheveled hair, who put her hands on his shoulders and gnashed her teeth. . . . With a single blow Khalid cracked open her head, and she was forthwith turned into a cinder."[11]

When Khalid Ibn al-Walid reported the incident to him, the prophet, who had been supervising the work of destruction, spoke the final word: "That's the end of Al-Uzza! After her there will be no more Al-Uzzas for the Arabs. For certain, she will no longer be worshipped after this day."[12]

Robbing woman of her reproductive power required the destruction of those on high who incarnated fecundity. The physical and verbal liquidation of the goddesses was an absolute necessity. One aspect of this liquidation is the metamorphosis of the sexual act, the most intimate relationship between man and woman, into an "opération à trois" involving man, woman, and God, with the last occupying the central position.

## Metamorphosis of the Sexual Act into an *Opération à Trois*: Appropriation of Orgasm by the Muslim God

The licit sexual act in Islam is not a sexual act between a man and a woman, but a sexual act that sets up a relationship between three beings: man, woman, and God. According to Bukhari, man must, at the moment of orgasm, pronounce the name of God. He explains the necessity for invoking the divine, at a moment when reason is faltering, by citing the presence of a fourth being, the devil (but we will soon see that in fact the devil is woman's double):

> The prophet said: Lo! If one of you, wanting to have intercourse with his wife, says, "In the name of God, keep the devil away from me, keep the devil away from the fruit of our union," and if then, fate or predestination causes a child to be born of these relations, the devil can never harm that child.[13]

Ghazzali goes a little further in his *Book of Good Practices as Regards Marriage*, advising that God be invoked not only at the moment of orgasm, but also at the beginning of the sexual act. He counsels the believer to prepare for committing himself to the arms of a woman by reciting some rather long, complicated prayers requiring a presence of mind, which, to say the least, is prejudicial to the concentration on the female body that such an act requires. Regarding good practices in intimate relations between spouses, he has this to say:

It is recommended that the husband begin by invoking the name of God and reciting Surah CXII, Verse 1 ("Say: He is Allah, the One!"), then the *takbir* and the *tahlil*,[14] and finally that he say: "In the name of God, the most High and the most Mighty, O God, see that it be a good posterity if thou hast decided to make one from my loins." The prophet (blessings on him) has said: "When one among you is going to know his wife, let him say: "O God, keep Satan away from me and keep Satan away from that which thou bestoweth on me as posterity." If then they beget a child, Satan will cause them no harm."

When ejaculation is near, it is advisable to recite silently without moving the lips these words: "Praise be to God, who created man from [a drop of] water," etc. (Surah XXV, Verse 54).[15]

Moreover, Ghazzali reports as an edifying example the case of a pious man who prayed so fervently at the moment of orgasm that his voice reverberated throughout the whole house.[16] Ghazzali also advises the believer to avoid facing Mecca during the sexual act "out of respect for the Kaaba," as if the sexual act were against God and his sanctuary.[17]

Like reproduction, it seems that the sexual act constituted a crisis situation for the Muslim God, a situation that he had to take over. He had to divert the believer's attention from the female body. He had to liquidate the body at hand, which offered pleasure and a child to man, and make present the absent — the God who could offer in concrete reality neither the one nor the other.

At least two institutions of the Muslim family can be viewed as attempts to disinvest the female body of the affective charge of desire and interest that man risks placing in it, repudiation and polygyny. These are mechanisms for the dissipation of man's affective investment in woman.[18] They constitute a negation of the couple as the basic unit of the Muslim family. The multiplicity of sexual partners that the Muslim family officially and institutionally puts at the disposal of the husband, whether through polygyny (up to four wives at a time) or through serial unions (repudiation permits the husband to dissolve a marriage verbally and unilaterally simply by pronouncing the words "You are repudiated") encourages the husband to make little emotional investment in a single woman, but rather to scatter his affective and emotional capacities.

The multiplicity of sexual partners for man is epitomized by the presence of the houri in paradisal space. She renders the presence of the earthly woman in Paradise (the ideal Muslim society) not only awkward, but seriously redundant, even superfluous. It is interesting to note that even the houri, however beautiful and perfect she is, does not escape the danger of multiplicity.

The descriptions of paradisal space quoted above leave a certain ambiguity regarding the number of houris due each believer. Does each have the right to only one houri or rather to several? If the Koran is amibiguous on this point, other texts are less so.

In the *Sahih*, Bukhari states that each believer has the right to two wives.[19] Al-Sindi, the commentator on Bukhari's text, finds fault with this statement, calling it an error. According to him, "the believer has the right to seventy-three wives, or something like that, and only God knows how many."[20]

Paradoxically Paradise, conceived as the male space par excellence, is invaded and physically occupied by the female element in the form of the houris.

Certain descriptions of the demographic disequilibrium of Paradise, especially those attributed to Al-Suyuti and Imam Ibn al-Qadi, have the ring of delirium.[21] When the believers reach the gates of Paradise, they are greeted by houris, each of whom holds a Koran; each houri steps forward and embraces her believer, declares her love for him, and retires with him to her house: "And in the house there are seventy beds. On each bed there are seventy cushions, and on each cushion a houri dressed in seventy gowns."[22]

The believer, who has just received a declaration of love from a houri eternally virginal, young, and beautiful, finds himself in her house literally swamped by 4,900 additional houris.

It is interesting to note that in the religious literature demographic disequilibrium in favor of the weaker sex — that is, a space taken over by women — is often tied to the images of hell and the end of the world.

The Prophet is supposed to have said, according to a *hadith* in Bukhari's *Sahih*:

> I was standing at the gate to Paradise. Most of those who entered were poor people, while the well-to-do were detained at the entrance (for the squaring of their account), with the exception of those who deserved hell and who had already been taken there. I stood at the gate of hell. Most of those who entered there were women.[23]

And again according to Bukhari, the Prophet is supposed to have mentioned an increase in the female population as a sign of the end of the world:

> I heard the messenger of God say: Among the precursory signs of the last hour will be the disappearance of science and the growth of ignorance; adultery will be more frequent; more wine will be drunk; the number of men will diminish, and women will become so numerous that there will only be one man to provide for fifty women.[24]

So we find, in a dizzying mirror effect, the absence of the couple and the multiplication of women around the believer (institutionalized by polygyny and repudiation) reflected in negative times and spaces like the end of the world and hell. It is necessary to understand how this ambiguous attitude toward the female as an encircling, swarming element is fostered by polygyny (as the basis of the order and happiness of the believer) and is identified at the same time as termination, destruction, and disorder (in the conceptions of the end of the world and hell). But this can only be done by situating it in its overall context — namely, the rewriting of desire in Muslim civilization, the substituting of one set of signs for another set.

## CASTRATION OF THE MALE BODY
## OF ITS CAPACITY TO DESIRE: THE PHALLUS MADE FETISH

We have already seen that the Muslim woman does not reproduce the race; it is God who creates the fetus and places it in her receptacle. In sterilizing woman, the Muslim God with the same stroke sterilized man. The child is not born of the sexual union of male believer and female believer. The child is born of the will of a third person, the divine person.

But castrating sexuality of its power to engender life leaves intact a dimension just as crucial — that of desire, of attraction to another body. Desire cuts man and woman off from the rest of the world and isolates them in their quest for orgasm. And orgasm is identified by the Muslim order as a sensation so strong, so enjoyable that it competes with the pleasures promised by God to the believer in Paradise:

> But truth to say, there is in concupiscence (*al-shahwa*) still another manifestation of divine wisdom, independent of its role in giving posterity to man. Indeed, when one satisfies it, one feels a sensual delight which would be peerless if only it were lasting. It is a foretaste of the delights which await one in Paradise, for promising man a delight which he had not tasted would be ineffective.[25]

And that is what makes it necessary for the divine to interfere here as well. The logic of sacred reality is that everything that brings pleasure on earth belongs to God. The divine is by definition monopolistic. The monotheistic God can only subjugate humans by controlling everything that brings them satisfaction, including their bodies; desire and the giving of life are two pleasures that are born of and take place through sexual union. The fury of the sacred order against the female body can only be explained by the fact that heterosexual union allies orgasm and procreation. Homosexual union, which is limited to orgasm, although forbidden by the Muslim order, is far from constituting a worry as major to the system as heterosexuality.[26] One can only understand the fundamentally misogynistic attitude of the sacred by placing it within the power struggle that God, the abstract body, and woman, the concrete body, wage every day. The sacred can be interpreted ultimately as a homosexual experience. It is the attempt of the male principle at self-fertilization, if one regards the monotheistic God as a projection of earthly man. The sacred is, among other things, the fertilization of earthly man by the male principle erected into a divine (that is, abstract) body. It is this that produces the fundamental conflict between heterosexual union and the sacred, which in Islam is focalized around the conflict between reason and desire. Since it cannot prevent heterosexual union on earth without destroying the human race, the sacred will try to drain it of its human dimension, the affective dimension. Islam integrates sexuality by lopping off its human dimension, desire.

*\* hence the male beloved of all mystical poetry*

**The Conflict between Reason and Desire**
**in the Muslim Order, or the Decapitation of Eros**
Islam is the religion of reason. It is organized around the concept of the believer
as a reasonable being capable of understanding and deciphering signs (al-ayat).
To be Muslim is first of all to understand God's signs, to decipher the ayat:

> 73. Allah . . . showeth you His portents so that ye may understand.
> 164. [these] are signs (of Allah's Sovereignty) for people who have sense.[27]
> (Surah II, "The Cow," p. 13 and p. 30)

Muslims are people who understand signs. In the Koran, *understanding* means
using one's reason. Orthographically, the Arabic words for *to understand* and
*reason* are indistinguishable.

This centering of Islam on reason ('aql) leads to defining under the broad
rubric of "desire" (shahwa) everything that risks deflecting the believer's attention
from his focal point, God, who is only accessible in and through the constant
exercise of reasoning. In order to illustrate this fundamental conflict of Muslim
civilization, which opposes civilization not to sexuality but to desire (which is
only a component of sexuality), we must skim through the treatises on love
and/or women. We must look at some examples of the discourse of chivalry in
our Muslim culture.[28]

There is a tendency for those who compare sexuality in Christian and Muslim
civilizations to succumb to hasty generalizations and especially to assert that
Islam has a positive attitude toward sexuality. This is true of Abdalwahad Bouhdiba,
who in his book, *La sexualité en islam*, never ceases congratulating himself as
a Muslim on the positive attitude of his civilization toward sexuality.[29] In fact,
you have to be a man, and a man with a special political conception of woman
and her place in society, to decode the Koranic message as a positive one regarding
sexuality and women. Islam does not have a positive attitude toward sexuality.
It has a fundamentally negative attitude toward it, as we have seen up to now
through the messages that it programs onto the female body. What distinguishes
it is its sophistication in the matter. Sexuality is not posed as totally contrary to
the order; it is posed as licit. But its most uncontrollable and versatile human
element, that which is richest in possibilities — desire — is at the same time
identified as the source and substance of the illicit. By connecting the licit (reason)
and the illicit (desire) we are going to find the key relational schema that we
identified in the preceding chapters — inversion-linkage. We will see that reason
and desire are linked in a power relationship where the strengthening of one is
inevitably accompanied by a weakening of the other. The achievement of equilibrium — that is, the triumph of reason — necessarily implies a constant struggle
that is never finally resolved.

In the discourse of chivalry, which tries to develop a theory of love, reason
('aql) is identified at the outset as the instrument of faith, of divine love: "God
has never been been worshipped by anything superior to reason."[30]

The same author carries this idea even further and makes reason the justification for and the prime quality of human existence: "Reason is the light of everything latent, beauty, of everything manifest; it is the foundation of order, the guide for the servant. Life has no meaning without it, and everything revolves around it."[31]

And he adds that a man's religion attains its fullness when his reason attains it also.[32]

Once reason has been identified as the key faculty of human existence, the basis of religion, and the essence of order, we are going to see the emergence of desire as the negative pole of the universe, the incarnation of the forces of disorder. Desire is the opposite of the divine will:

> Allah made desire the opposite (mudaddun) of the message that he entrusted to his prophet. For God, following one's desire is equivalent (muaqbilan) to forsaking the message of his prophets. God has thus divided people into two groups: those who follow inspiration (al-wahy) and those who follow desire (al-hawa). And this split is clear in various Koranic verses, like the one that says: "And if they answer thee not, then know that what they follow is their lusts."[33]

The verse that Ibn Qayyim al-Jawzia quotes is Verse 50 of Surah XXVIII, "The Story," which clearly illustrates the fundamental opposition between God and desire: "And if they answer thee not, then know that what they follow is their lusts. And who goeth farther astray than he who followeth his lust without guidance from Allah. . . ."

It is around the Koranic verses concerning the conflict between God and desire that the theoreticians of the discourse of chivalry articulate their theory of love. The same author as above, relying on Koranic verses, poses the fundamental distinction in Muslim civilization, the distinction between human and animal. A man who pursues his desires renounces his civilized aspect and falls to the state of an animal:

> God . . . compared those who pursued their lusts to the animals who were ugliest in form and concept. One time he compared them to dogs in a verse which reads: ". . . but he clung to the earth and followed his own lust. Therefore his likeness is as the likeness of a dog." In another verse he compared them to asses: "As they were frightened asses fleeing from a lion." Finally, in other instances God transformed them into monkeys and pigs.[34]

The author of Rawdat al-muhibbin (The Lovers' Garden), Ibn Qayyim al-Jawzia, explains the intrinsically polluting character of desire (al-hawa). If it touches science, it transforms it into bid'a (innovation) and thus into errant behavior (dalala); if it touches power and him who exercises it, it corrupts both and puts them in the service of injustice. And finally, if desire touches the leader of the Muslim community, it transforms him into a traitor to the cause of Islam, making him govern against its laws and instructions.[35] For another writer, Imam Abd al-Rahman Ibn al-Jawzi, "there is no sleep deeper than inattention (al-ghafla), and no slavery more total than desire. And without deep inattention, desire can never triumph over you."[36] Reason and desire are connected in a power relationship, and any strengthening of one implies the weakening of the other. This inversion-linkage is the key relational schema that organizes the sacred universe and is condensed in the following formulations: "If desire triumphs, the capacity for discernment (al-ra'i) disappears"[37]; "The man who has the strongest will is he who triumphs over his desire."[38]

Will (al-'azm) and discernment (al-ra'i), which are aspects of reason, work together in the struggle against desire (al-hawa): "If reason governs, desire surrenders (salamahu al-hawa) and becomes its servant and slave. And if desire governs, reason becomes its prisoner. It submits to it."[39]

According to Imam Ibn al-Jawzi, the struggle against desire was identified by the prophet as being the "great jihad," the holy war, in contrast with the "small jihad," which is the physical war against the enemies of Islam.[40] He who triumphs over his desires and masters them has the mental and physical strength of ten and takes his place in the scale of values above the mujahid, the warrior who conquers a whole godless town.[41]

The cardinal virtue in the Muslim system of values, muruwa, is loyalty to all that the system imposes as sacred and inviolable, especially the fulfillment of its duties, that is, strict and unfailing conformity of behavior to the divine will and its laws. And muruwa is regarded as imposing, among other duties, resistance to desire.[42] The Prophet is supposed to have said that a man's strength "is not measured by his capacity to vanquish other men, but by his capacity to vanquish his own self (nafsahu)."[43] Al-hawa, desire, is the source of all anomalies and abnormal developments (al-balaa'), and the struggle against desire is the sole way of checking them and reestablishing the norm, health.[44]

Once al-hawa, a vague and general concept, has been established as the subversive pole of the Muslim order, the source of destruction, lack of reason, and abnormality, our writers are going to specifically identify it as being temptation in two indissociable forms: the devil and woman. We have seen that reason is regarded as the instrument of divine worship: "Nothing disarms Satan like a reasoning believer."[45] And the will of this reasoning believer, so incorruptible when face to face with Satan, crumbles when Satan allies himself with a woman: "When Satan despairs of someone, he tries to use women as intermediaries."[46] With Ibn al-Jawzi, the overlap is complete; female beauty is a manifestation of the devil: "Man's looking upon the beauty of women is one of the poisoned arrows of Iblis (the devil)."[47]

According to the same author, Iblis is supposed to have said: "The surest arrow that I have, the one which never misses its victim, is woman."[48]

This identification of the desire/devil/woman triad is very clear in religious literature. But authors such as Ibn Qayyim al-Jawzia and Ibn al-Jawzi, who took upon themselves the task of explaining love, present this to the believer as a fact of the sacred system and not as a very carefully worked out theory of desire.

For Bukhari, whose aim in writing the *Sahih* was to establish the rigorous authenticity of the *hadiths* (the traditions attributed to the prophet), the identification of woman as the danger pole and the incarnation of disorder is plain. According to one of the *hadiths*: "The Prophet said: 'I will not leave after me any cause of trouble more fatal to man than women.'"

Imam Muslim asserts the same thing in his *Sahih*. According to him, the prophet saw a woman in the street, hastened home and had sexual intercourse with his wife, Zaynab, and later joined his companions to whom he said: "Woman comes in the form of a Satan and she leaves in the form of a Satan. When one of you sees a woman, he must hasten to his own woman. By doing this, he regains his wits (*yaruddu ma fi nafsihi*)."[50]

Imam Muslim comments on this *hadith* and explains that the prophet, by giving this advice and by comparing woman to the devil, is referring to desire and to the incitement to disorder represented by woman, who is for men "a constant temptation because of the pleasure she gives them, whether through a mere look or through all that concerns her." He concluded by saying that she is compared to the devil because she incites to evil (*al-sharr*).[51]

Ghazzali, whose analytical approach has an admirable rigor, summarizes the identification of the diabolic with the female in a concise and clear expression: "When a man's penis is in erection, he loses a third of his reason. Others say that he loses a third of his religion." And he explains this phenomenon by opposing reason to desire. According to him, erection is a test of man's will, which reduces it to nothing, for when desire flares up, reason cannot control it.[52]

From this comes the necessity to control woman, to neutralize her as much as possible, for she is the unique concrete incarnation of desire. The devil, like God, has no physical existence. Mastering woman means mastering desire. Subjugating woman means the triumph of reason, the divine will, and order. Marriage, according to Ghazzali, is slavery (*riqq*).[53] The supremacy of man over woman means the supremacy of reason over unreason. Ghazzali, so conscious of the equality of all persons before God as a principle of the Muslim order, decides on a limit to the logic of that principle: "The Prophet said: If I had to order one being to bow down before another, I would require woman to prostrate herself before her husband because of the magnitude of what she owes him."[54] For a man to obey a woman would be to reverse the order; it would be to install disorder, explains Ghazzali.[55]

And it is the necessity to subjugate woman as the incarnation of desire, the necessity for the believer to dominate and master her that explains the fundamentally misogynistic attitude of Islam, which is very plain in legal Islam and especially in the *Sahihs*. Misogyny — contempt for women and discrimination against them — is a structural characteristic and a pivotal axis of the Muslim order; the reason/desire conflict overlays and polarizes a whole series of conflicts, each one as determining as the other:

| The male principle represents: | The female principle represents: |
|:---:|:---:|
| Reason | Desire |
| Order | Disorder |
| God | Devil |
| Control | The Uncontrollable |

The relationship at the heart of each of these binomials is inversion-linkage, a power relationship in which equilibrium is only achieved by a constant struggle against the forces of disequilibrium. God, order, and reason are never permanent acquirements; they are only the outcome of constant struggles between opposing forces. This is what leads to the idea of equilibrium, which is fundamental in the perception of sacred time. In sacred time there is no such thing as process, an initial combination of elements that is transformed into a new combination, different from the initial combination but not necessarily opposed to it. In sacred time no change is possible without it resulting in disequilibrium. From among an array of possible combinations of opposing forces, God, reason, and order are only one potential result. But any attack on this precise combination, which alone represents "equilibrium," can bring nothing but disequilibrium. From this comes the identification of change as *bid'a*, as errant behavior. This also makes it necessary for the believer to remain on the *qui vive* with the being with whom he shares the most profound intimacy possible in a licit context (homosexuality being condemned as illicit): a woman.

In order for the equilibrium between reason and desire to be achievable during sexual relations, it is necessary, in addition to invoking the name of God before and during orgasm, to fetishize the female body, to liquidate desire, to excise the affective and the emotional in order to safeguard the intellect, the faculty of reasoning.

Paradoxically it is because woman is recognized as too important to man that the Muslim God obliges man (so that he can worship God without the shadow of a rival) to fetishize her, to reduce her to a mere heap of organs that can be brought to orgasm by conscious and deliberate manipulation. This is what produces the very special nature of eroticism in the orthodox discourse. It is an eroticism without desire, one that must destroy, or at least minimize, emotional investment and concentrate on investment in the body. The ideal sexual relationship must not be a relationship between a man and a woman, capable of mobilizing their affective, intellectual, and sensual resources in order to maximize the quality of the pleasure they can share. The ideal sexual relationship should be manipulation of the body as a synthesis of organs stripped of affective content and polarized around the genitals.[56]

### The Castrated Believer's Reward: The Phallus Made Fetish

Once desire as a component of sexual relations between a man and woman has been meticulously excised, the Muslim God goes on to encourage his doubly castrated believer (we have seen that the believer does not reproduce either) to apply himself without restraint to that fetishized and fetishizing sexuality. The most perfect expression of this phenomenon is the famous Verse 223 of the Surah entitled "The Cow," where the female vagina is depicted as a field and the penis as a working tool:

> 223. Your women are a tilth for you (to cultivate) so go to your tilth as ye will, and send (good deeds) before you for your souls. . . .
>
> (Surah II, "The Cow," pp. 43-44)

Imam Muslim's *Sahih* (in an analysis adopted moreover by other *Sahihs*) explains the very special context of this verse. According to Imam Muslim, this verse came to clarify the doubt in people's minds about the positions for coitus permitted by Islam. He writes that the Jewish tribes believed that when a man took his wife from behind (it is carefully explained that penetration must be into the vagina and not the anus), the resulting child risked being cross-eyed.[57] Other *hadiths* reported that this verse had come to solve the problem posed by inter-marriages between Muhammad's tribe, the Quraysh, and the Ansar tribe, the tribe of Medina, where the prophet was exiled after the Hegira. A woman of the Ansar, married to a Quraysh, is supposed to have refused to lend herself to the whims of her husband who wanted to make love from behind. She insisted that in her tribe the man could only make love to a woman lying on her side. The conflict became so heated that it was submitted to the prophet for decision. He replied by the verse under discussion and, according to Ibn Dawud, is supposed to have commented on it by explaining that a man can take his wife in any position whatever, "from the front, from behind, lying on the side."[58]

This verse epitomizes the result of a whole detailed programming of sexuality, drained of its affective dimension and reduced to organic manipulation, to simple bodily exercises in which the male sexual organ will be invested with an almost magical force.

The Muslim man must be able to emulate and model himself on *the* standard of male vigor — the prophet Muhammad himself: "According to Anas, the Prophet in one single night visited his wives, and he had nine (at that time)."[59]

The best man of the Muslim nation is "he who has the most wives."[60] Hassan Ibn Ali, the grandson of the prophet, who had a notorious tendency to increase the number of his marriages (he is credited with 200 wives), is supposed to have been particularly approved of, encouraged, and admired by the prophet.[61]

And it is here that we find one of the fundamental differences between the religious erotic discourse and the orthodox discourse. According to the religious erotic discourse, as we have seen in Part I of this book, the orgasmic capacity of the vagina is unlimited. By contrast the penis is presented as incapable of responding to it; man as a lover, as a sexual being, is presented as inferior to his partner in physical stamina and potency. In the orthodox discourse, on the contrary, we witness a magnifying of the power of the phallus. Man's sexual appetite is described as being unlimited, and the problem posed by the *fuqahas* (scholars of religious science) as a threat to Muslim marriage is the inability of the wife to respond to the sexual appetite of her vigorous husband. The premise behind the debates of the imams in the *Sahihs* and the *Sunnas* is that the sexual appetite of the believer is quite simply fabulous. Muslim marriage and family laws are organized around this belief. How to prevent this supersexed believer from illicitly fornicating is the question that preoccupies the Muslim legislator. How is the believer to be induced to be satisfied with licit relations? Polygyny and repudiation are justified as being the answers to this problem:

> As for him, on the other hand, who is particularly assailed by that passion [carnal passion] and for whom one single woman is not enough to preserve chastity, to him it is recommended that he take other wives in addition to the first one, up to four in all. If God, through his will and grace, thus makes his life easy and he has a tranquil heart through them (it is well and good). If not, change is recommended to him. . . . It is said that Hassan Ibn Ali was a great one for marrying; he married, in all, more than two hundred wives; sometimes he took four at a time; sometimes he repudiated all of his wives at the same time and took others in their place. Muhammad (peace and blessings on him) said to Hassan: "You resemble me physically and morally."[62]

Since fornication is forbidden, the Muslim man must not only guard against it by increasing the number of legitimate wives, but also by changing them through repudiation as soon as he feels boredom creeping into his relationship with his partners.[63]

So the problem is to make certain that this exceptionally powerful sexual appetite of the believer finds satisfaction within lawful limits. The *fuqahas* then are going to get into the details of the sexual act; it will be minutely spelled out.

There must be no unnecessary restraints to interfere with the prowess in bed of this supersexed believer. The imams unanimously affirmed that all positions were permitted with the exception of sodomy.[64] And must man abstain from intercourse during menstruation? They answered this question in full detail, including what he should do if the wife refuses to make love. "*Al-nushuz*," the refusal of the wife to engage in the sexual act, becomes a very serious crime: "The Prophet said: When a husband calls his wife to his bed and she refuses to come, the angels curse her until morning."[65]

And Tarmidi assures the wife who does not refuse her husband that "every wife who passes the night at the side of her satisfied husband is sure to go to Paradise."[66]

At no point in the orthodox discourse do the imams pose the opposite problem: the case of a wife who has an appetite that surpasses that of her husband and so remains sexually unsatisfied. In sacred reality, the sexual act is not an act between two equal beings. It is an act concerning only one person, the believer of the male sex; his physical satisfaction is the aim. The objective of Muslim family laws is to assure the believer's access to this pleasure, which must be strictly physical. The women, whose number he can increase within the framework of the law as much as he wants through repudiation and polygyny, are nothing but interchangeable fetishes. Their function is to permit him to achieve an orgasmic release as mechanical as possible in order to free him for the fundamental relationship — that with God. The function of marriage in Islam is clearly laid out by Ghazzali, who in his *Revival of the Science of Religion* elaborated the most brilliant theory of sexuality that can be found in the religious literature. For him, man's essential allegiance is to God; God is his raison d'être. But in order for a man to be able to concentrate on God and worship him, he has to settle the problem of the physical tension of sexual excitement and do that in as summary a way as possible. Any psychic investment by him in sexual relations would be a very serious danger, for it would reverse the divine order, which demands that woman be inferior to man and be fixed at the level of a fetish, the merely physical:

> The soul quickly tires of doing its duty because duty is against its nature. If one forces it to do what it is loath to do, it rebels. But if, now and then, the soul can find relaxation through a few pleasures, it is strengthened and becomes ready for work. It is in the familiar company of women that one finds that relaxation which chases away sadness and gives rest to the heart. It is desirable for pious souls to find refreshment through that which is permitted by religion.[67]

Islam is not a construction of the universe whose objective is to permit the human being to actualize his potentialities. Its objective is to take some of a person's potentialities and from them fashion a believer, who is to be a being totally committed to obedience to and worship of a superior, abstract force: God. He is only fulfilled within that unequal relationship. Like woman, man's end is not in himself. He is only defined by relation to the need of another. Woman is defined by relation to the orgasmic need of the male believer. The believer is defined by relation to God's need to be worshipped.

# 13 Conclusion: Female Beauty as a Mirror of the Male Condition

The ideal of female beauty in Islam is obedience, silence, and immobility, that is, inertia and passivity. These are far from being trivial characteristics nor are they limited to women. In fact, these three attributes of female beauty are the three qualities of the believer vis-à-vis his God. The believer must dedicate his life to obeying and worshipping God and abiding by his will.

The believer comes into a world organized and programmed beforehand by divine power, and God explicitly requires him to be passive. Any manifestation of will by the believer, any attempt to change the existing order, to create alternatives is *bida'*, innovation, and this is errant behavior. The source of the orthodox discourse is the Koran, which is the discourse of the superior one, God. The voice of the believer cannot make itself heard without destabilizing the equilibrium of the system and perverting the order. Man must invest his energy, not in attempts to express himself, but in attempts to decipher the discourse of the almighty. This is the objective of religious science. The *fuqahas* and imams devote themselves to the task essential to the lives of individuals and the *umma*: interpreting the will of the other and abiding by it. The believer is fulfilled not by expressing himself, but by making his own the expression of the other, the superior one, God.

The silent believer is also inert, without will. We have seen how, at the level of economics, nature has been created for him according to a precise divine plan, and all he must do in this earthly life is to pray to God, to worship him day and night in order to receive the goods which he needs.

In the sacred universe the believer is fashioned in the image of woman — deprived of speech and will and committed to obedience to another. The female condition and the male condition are not different in the end to which they are directed, but in the pole around which they orbit. The lives of beings of the male sex revolve around the divine will. The lives of beings of the female sex revolve around the will of believers of the male sex. And in both cases the human element, in terms of multiple unforeseeable potentialities, must be liquidated in order to bring about the triumph of the sacred, the triumph of the divine — that is, the nonhuman, passivity and inertia.

# Notes

## CHAPTER 1

1. Imam Ghazzali, *Ihya' 'ulum al-din* (Cairo: Al-Maktaba al-Tijariya al-Kubra, n.d.).
2. This is not meant to suggest that these characteristics are exclusive to Islam. The *"soi belle et tais toi"* attitude in sophisticated France and the "dumb blond" image in profit-making, much less sophisticated Hollywood, are well known. I refrain from pointing out the comparisons because I trust the readers to make their own comparisons as long as the Muslim model is shaped with crystal clarity.
3. M. Merleau-Ponty, *Phenomenology of Perception* (London: Routledge & Kegan Paul, 1962), p. 154.

## CHAPTER 2

1. The English translation used is the following: *The Glorious Koran*, a Bilingual Edition with English Translation, Introduction and Notes by Marmaduke Pickthall (Albany: State University of New York Press, 1976). All Koranic quotations and citations are from this edition.
2. Imam Malik, *Al-Muwatta* (Beirut: Mansurat Dar al-Afaq al-Jadida, 1979).
3. Imam Bukhari, *Al-Sahih* (Beirut: Dar al-Ma'rifa, n.d.).
4. Imam Muslim, *Al-Sahih* (Beirut: Al-Maktab al-Tijari lil-Tib'a wal Nashr, n.d.).
5. Tarmidi, *Al-Sunan* (Medina: Matba'at al-Kutbi, Al-Maktaba al-Salafiya, n.d.).
6. Louis Milliot, *Introduction à l'étude du droit musulman* (Paris: Sirey, 1953), p. 103.
7. Ibid., p. 106.
8. Ibid., p. 107.
9. Ibid., p. 110.
10. See Chapter 4, Notes 2, 3, and 4.
11. Salah al-Munajid, *Al-Hayat al-jinsiya 'ind al-Arab* (Beirut: Dar al-Kitab, 1958).
12. Ibid., pp. 102 ff.
13. Ibid. p. 100.
14. Ibid.
15. Ibid. p. 101.
16. Abdelwahab Bouhdiba, *La sexualité en islam* (Paris: Presses Universitaires de France, 1975). See particularly the Introduction.
17. A few of the works classified by Al-Munajid as manuscripts have since been published.
18. Imam Abd al-Rahman al-Suyuti, *Al-Rahma fil-tibb wal-hikma* (Beirut: Al-Maktaba al-Thaqafiya, n.d.).
    Abu Bakr al-Azraq, *Tashil al-manafi' fil-tibb wal-hikma* (Beirut: Al-Matba'a al-Sa'biya, n.d.).
19. Al-Jahid, *Al-Rasa'il* (Maktabat al-Khanji, 1964), "Kitab al-Qiyan" and "Mufakharat al-jawari wal-ghilman."
20. Ibn Hazm, *Tuq al-hamama* (Beirut: Dar Maktabat al-Hayat, 1976). (Author born 994, died 1014 A.D.)

119

Shaykh Ibn al-Husayn al-Sarraj, *Masari' al-'ushaq* (Beirut: Dar Masadir, n.d.). (Author born 1026, died 1106 A.D.)

Imam Abd al-Rahman Ibn al-Jawzi, *Dhamm al-hawa* (Publisher not indicated, 1962).

Ibn Qayyim al-Jawzia, *Rawdat al-muhibbin wa nuzhat al-mushtaqin* (Beirut: Dar al-Kitab al-'ilmiyya, 1977).

Dawud al-Antaqi, *Tazyin al-ashwaq fi akhbar al-'ushaq* (Beirut: Dar Ahmad Mayhu, 1973). (This book was written in 972 A.H.)

Shihab al-Din Ibn Hajla al-Maghrabi, *Diwan al-sababa* (Beirut: Dar Ahmad Mayhu, 1973).

Jalal al-Din al-Suyuti, *Kitab al-mustatrif fi akhbar al-jawari* (Beirut: Dar al-Kitab al-Jadid, 1976). (The author died in 911 A.H.)

Imam Abu Tahir Tayfur, *Balaghat al-nisa'* (Beirut: Dar al-Nahda al-Haditha, 1972).

Ibn Qayyim al-Jawzia, *Akhbar al-nisa'* (Beirut: Dar Maktabat al-Hayat, 1973). (Author born 691 A.H.)

21. Al-Tuhami Gannun al-Idrisi al-Hasani, *Qurrat al-'uyun fil-niqa al-sahra'i wa adabuh*, 3rd ed. (Dar al-'Ilm lil-Jami', 1964). (The publisher's name means "House of Science for the Masses.")

Nasir al-Din al-Albani, *Adab al-zifaf fil-sunna al-tahira*, 4th ed. (Beirut: Al Maktab al-Islami, n.d.).

22. Ibn Ahmad al-Qadi, *Daqa'iq al-akhbar fi dhikr al-janna wal-nar* (Casablanca: Dar al-Tib'a al-Haditha, n.d.).

Jalal al-Din al-Suyuti, *Al-durar al hisan fil-ba'th wa na'im al-jinan*. (This work is usually printed with the preceding one.)

Imam Ghazzali, *Al-durra al-fakhira fi kashaf 'ulum al-akhira* (Cairo: Maktabat al-Jundi Sayyidna al-Husayn, n.d.). An English translation of this work by Jane Idleman Smith, under the title *The Precious Pearl*, appeared in 1979 (Missoula, Montana: Scholars Press).

23. Jean Baudrillard, *Pour une critique de l'économie politique du signe* (Paris: Gallimard, 1972), "Fétichisme et idéologie," pp. 110 ff.

## CHAPTER 3

1. This implication is clearly demonstrated by Fatima Mernissi in "Women and the Impact of Capitalist Development in Morocco," a two-part article appearing in *Feminist Issues* 2, no. 2, pp. 69-104, and *Feminist Issues* 3, no. 1, pp. 61–112.

2. David C. Gordon, *Women of Algeria: An Essay on Change*, Harvard Middle East Monographs, no. 19 (Cambridge: Harvard University Press, 1968), p. 77.

3. Gregory Massell, *The Surrogate Proletariat: Moslem Women and Revolutionary Strategies in Soviet Central Asia: 1919–1929* (Princeton: Princeton University Press, 1974).

4. Wilhelm Reich, *The Sexual Revolution* (New York: Farrar, Strauss and Giroux, 1945).

5. Hilda Scott, *Does Socialism Liberate Women?* (Boston: Beacon Press, 1974).

6. C. K. Yang, *Chinese Communist Society: The Family and the Village* (Cambridge, Mass.: MIT Press, 1959).

7. Eugene Genovese, *Roll, Jordan, Roll: The World the Slaves Made* (New York: Pantheon, 1974).
8. Julia Cherry Spruill, *Women's Life and Work in the Southern Colonies* (New York: Norton, 1972). (Originally published in 1938.)
   Peter Laslett, *Family Life and Illicit Love in Earlier Generations* (London: Cambridge University Press, 1977), Chapter 7, "Household and Family on the Slave Plantations of the U.S.A.," pp. 233–60.
9. One of the analyses that still remains pertinent is: Wilhelm Reich, *The Mass Psychology of Fascism* (New York: Farrar, Strauss and Giroux, 1970).
10. Reimut Reich, *Sexualité et lutte de classes* (Paris: Maspero, 1971).
    Betty Friedan, *The Feminine Mystique* (New York: Dell Publishers, 1963).
11. Michel Foucault, *The History of Sexuality, Volume I, An Introduction* (New York: Vintage Books, 1980). (Originally published in French as *Histoire de la sexualité I, La volonté de savoir* [Paris: Gallimard, 1976].)
12. Ester Boserup, *Women's Role in Economic Development* (New York: St. Martin's Press, 1970).
13. "Review and Evaluation of Progress Achieved in the Implementation of the World Plan for Action: Employment," World Conference of the United Nations Decade for Women, Copenhagen, 14–30 July 1980 (A/Conf./.94/8).
    "Review and Evaluation of Progress Achieved in the Implementation of the World Plan for Action: Education," World Conference of the United Nations Decade for Women, Copenhagen, 14–30 July 1980 (A/Conf./.94/10).
    "Effective Mobilization of Women in Development: Report of the Secretary General," United Nations Document A/33/238 and corr. rep.
    Dipack Mazundar, "The Urban Informal Sector," World Bank Reprints Series, no. 43, August 1976.
14. Claude Meillassoux, *Femmes, greniers et capitaux* (Paris: Maspero, 1975).
15. For a recent analysis of the future trends of the Arab economy in general and of employment in particular, see the documents presented by the Arab experts at the symposium entitled "The Arab World in the Year 2000," organized by the Arab States Regional Bureau of the United Nations Development Program and held at Tangier 5–8 May 1980.
    In his book, *The Arab Economy Today* (London: Zed Press, 1982), Samir Amin says that "the Arab economy is more externally oriented — and hence more dependent — than the economies of the rest of the Third World" (p. 51). This book was originally published under the title *L'économie arabe contemporaine* (Paris: Minuit, 1980).
16. A conspiracy of silence surrounds prostitution as an aspect of economic dependence, at the international as much as at the local level. A recent documentation of prostitution and its international ramifications is that of Kathleen Barry, who made particular use of INTERPOL documents. See Kathleen Barry, *Female Sexual Slavery* (Englewood Cliffs, New Jersey: Prentice-Hall, 1979), Chapter 4, "The Traffic in Sexual Slaves," pp. 45–72.
17. See Fatima Mernissi, "Women and the Impact of Capitalist Development in Morocco."
18. See: Fatima Mernissi, *Beyond the Veil* (Cambridge, Mass.: Schenkman Publishing Company, 1975), Chapter 9, "The Economic Basis of Sexual Anomie in Modern Morocco," pp. 89–97.

19. G. Balandier, *Anthropo-logiques* (Paris: Presses Universitaires de France, 1974), Chapter 1, "Hommes et femmes ou la moitié dangereuse," pp. 13–61.

## CHAPTER 4

1. See Salah al-Munajid, *Al-Hayat al-jinsiya 'ind al-Arab* (Sexual Life Among the Arabs); and Abdelwahab Bouhdiba, *La sexualité en islam*, Chapter XI, "Erotologie."
2. The title in Arabic is *Al-Raud al-'atir wa nuzhat al-khatir* (publisher's name not specified). The English translation used here is the famous translation by Sir Richard Burton (originally published in 1876) in the following edition: *The Perfumed Garden of the Shaykh Nefzawi*, translated by Sir Richard Burton and edited with an introduction and additional notes by Alan Hull Walton (London: Neville Spearman, 1963). For passages not included by Burton in his translation, the versions used here are translated from the French edition (and so indicated by reference to it): *La prairie parfumée où s'ébattent les plaisirs*, trans. René Khawam (Paris: Editions Phebus, 1976).
3. The title in Arabic is *Ruju' al-shaykh ila sabah fil-quwwa ala al-bah* (publisher's name not specified). Selections from this book have been translated and published in French in the following edition: *Le livre de la volupté pour que le vieillard recouvre sa jeunesse* (Paris: Editions Sycomore, 1979). An English translation in two volumes, entitled *The Old Man Young Again*, was published by Charles Carrington in Paris in 1898. The edition was limited to 500 sets and is virtually unobtainable now. The quotations from this work used here, however, have been translated from the original Arabic into French by the author, and then into English by the English translator.
4. René Khawam gives the fifteenth century as the date for the original composition of *The Perfumed Garden*. Burton believed that it was written in the beginning of the sixteenth century, about the year 925 of the Hegira, but Alan Hull Walton says that recent investigations indicate that it was probably written between the years 1394 and 1433.
5. *The Perfumed Garden*, p. 75.
6. Ibid., p. 76.
7. *How An Old Man Can Regain His Youth*, p. 3.
8. *The Perfumed Garden*, p. 182.

## CHAPTER 5

1. *The Perfumed Garden*, p. 97.
2. Erich Neumann, *The Great Mother, An Analysis of the Archetype* (Princeton: Princeton University Press, 1963), Chapter III, "The Two Characters of the Feminine," pp. 24 ff.
   J. J. Bachofen, *Myth, Religion, and Mother Right* (Princeton: Princeton University Press, 1967), pp. 69 ff.
3. *The Perfumed Garden*, p. 96.
4. *How An Old Man Can Regain His Youth*, p. 37.
5. Ibid., p. 57.
6. *The Glorious Koran*, Surah LIII, "The Star," Verses 19–23. See my discussion of the destruction of the Arab goddesses in Chapter 12.

7. *The Perfumed Garden*, p. 201.
8. Ibid., p. 72.
9. *La prairie parfumée*, p. 215.
10. *The Perfumed Garden*, pp. 187, 191.
11. Ibid., pp. 189, 190.
12. *How An Old Man Can Regain His Youth*, p. 72.
13. Ibid.
14. Ibid.
15. *La prairie parfumée*, p. 215.
16. *How An Old Man Can Regain His Youth*, p. 103.
17. *La prairie parfumée*, p. 200.
18. *How An Old Man Can Regain His Youth*, p. 94.
19. Ibid.
20. Ibid., p. 105.
21. Ibid., pp. 79, 77, 73, 81.
22. *The Glorious Koran*, Surah IV, "Women," Verse 3.
23. *The Glorious Koran*, Surah XII, "Joseph," Verse 28. The female destructive power, the *qaid*, is the substructure of Muslim Arab North African folklore, as can be seen in collections of tales and proverbs.

## CHAPTER 6

1. *How An Old Man Can Regain His Youth*, pp. 95–96.
2. A *wali* is a legal guardian. A woman does not marry in Muslim society, but the wali, a man who is the father or his representative on earth, gives her in marriage. For more on this subject see the following: Imam Malik, *Kitab al-muwatta*, section on "The views of the virgin and the nonvirgin on their marriage," pp. 484 ff.; Imam Bukhari, *Al-Sahih*, vol. 3, chapter on marriage, p. 250; Imam Muslim, *Al-Sahih*, vol. 3, p. 140; Tarmidi, *Al-Sahih*, vol. 2, p. 380.
3. *Jabr* means compulsion. On the right of the father to compel his children of both sexes, but especially his daughter, to marry, see the works cited in Note 2. This right of compulsion is far from being unanimously accepted; there are those who contest it. A concise summary of both positions can be found in Milliot, *Introduction à l'étude du droit musulman*, p. 295.
4. *Kafa'* means social homogeneity. Like the wali and *jabr*, *kafa'* is a key concept of the Muslim family as an institution. In addition to the works cited in Note 2, see the very concise summary, entitled "Mésalliance," by Milliot in his *Introduction à l'étude du droit musulman*, p. 293. To appreciate the quandary of contemporary jurists regarding the concept of *kafa'*, which is in flagrant contradiction with the principle of equality among believers, one should read the position taken by Qadi Mikou in his recent treatise, where he gives an explanation of the *muduwana* (register) of personal status: *Al-Wasit* (Rabat: Matbaat Kawthar, 1971), pp. 218–28.
5. Reported in Mikou, *Al-Wasit*, p. 221.
6. For example, the *muduwana* (register) of personal status promulgated in Morocco by a Dahir of 1957 stipulates in Article 14, in a formula which is ambiguity itself, that for clarifications regarding the notion of *kafa'*, one should refer to '*urf*, that is, customs. In a country like Morocco, as in all other Muslim countries, where inequality

and social hierarchization make up the fundamental models that rule relations between individuals and where matrimonial manipulations as power strategies are "customs," one can imagine the impact of such legal dispositions on any project for democracy.

7. *The Perfumed Garden*, pp. 203–4.
8. *How An Old Man Can Regain His Youth*, pp. 79–80.
9. See for instance: Allal al-Fassi, Al-Akkad, etc.
10. *How An Old Man Can Regain His Youth*, pp. 100–101.
11. *The Perfumed Garden*, p. 110.
12. Ibid., pp. 109–10.
13. Ibid., p. 107.
14. Ibid., p. 111.
15. Ibid., p. 112.
16. Ibid., p. 115.
17. See the sexual dynamics in the *Arabian Nights*.
18. The discourse of the marvelous refers here only to the *Arabian Nights*. The author's original plan was to decode the messages tattooed on women's bodies by four discourses in Arab Muslim culture: orthodox Islam, Sufi Islam, the literature of the marvelous, and religious erotic literature. The enormity of the task made it necessary to present the material in more than one book.
19. *The Glorious Koran*, Surah XXIV, "Light," Verse 2, p. 456.
20. *The Perfumed Garden*, pp. 85, 94.
21. Ibid., p. 88.
22. *La prairie parfumée*, p. 81.
23. *The Perfumed Garden*, pp. 92, 94.
24. *How An Old Man Can Regain His Youth*, p. 98.
25. *The Perfumed Garden*, p. 104.
26. Ibid., p. 250. (In the relation of this incident, Burton's nonstandard transliteration of Arabic names has been retained. — Trans.)
27. Ibid., p. 257.
28. Ibid., p. 258.
29. Ibid.
30. Ibid., pp. 257, 258, 259.
31. *La prairie parfumée*, p. 271.
32. See the following chapters.
33. *The Perfumed Garden*, p. 224.
34. Ibid., p. 112.
35. *How An Old Man Can Regain His Youth*, p. 75.
36. Ibid., p. 81.
37. Ibid.

## CHAPTER 7

1. The Tent-Pole Man is a man whose penis, in a constant state of erection, holds out his robe the way a tent-pole holds up a tent.
2. Serge Moscovici, *La société contre nature* (Paris: Union Génerale d'Editions, 1972), p. 283.
3. Abbas Mahmud al-Akkad, *Al mar'a fil-quran* (Beirut: Dar al-Kitab al-Arabi, 1967).

4. *The Perfumed Garden*, pp. 124–26.
5. *How An Old Man Can Regain His Youth*, p. 61. Al-Alfiya is supposed to have written an important illustrated erotic treatise that played a great role in inspiring the producers and consumers of this literature in Arab society, especially the kings. See Al-Munajid, *Sexual Life Among the Arabs*, p. 105.
6. *The Perfumed Garden*, p. 214.
7. Ibid., p. 107–108.
8. *La prairie parfumée*, p. 138.
9. *How An Old Man Can Regain His Youth*, p. 113.
10. *The Perfumed Garden*, pp. 157–59.
11. Ghazzali, *The Revival of the Science of Religion*, chapter on marriage, p. 34.
12. *How An Old Man Can Regain His Youth*, p. 41.
13. Ibid.
14. "They invoke in his [Allah's] stead only females" (*The Glorious Koran*, Surah IV, Verse 117).
15. *The Perfumed Garden*, p. 127.
16. *How An Old Man Can Regain His Youth*, p. 68.
17. Ibid.
18. Ibid., p. 111.
19. Ibid., pp. 63–68.
20. Ibid., p. 64.
21. Ibid., p. 87.
22. Ibid., p. 88.
23. *The Perfumed Garden*, p. 163.
24. *La prairie parfumée*, p. 232.
25. *The Perfumed Garden*, pp. 157–58.
26. Al-Suyuti, *Al-Rahma fil-tibb wal-hikma* (Beirut: Al-Maktaba al-Taqafiya, n.d.), p. 165.
27. Ibid., p. 166.
28. Shaykh al-Imam Ibrahim Ibn Abd al-Rahman Ibn Abi Bakr al-Azraq, *Tashil al-manafi' fil-tibb wal-hikma* (Beirut: Al-Maktaba al-Sa'bia, n.d.).
29. Ibid., p. 74.
30. Ibid., p. 133.
31. *How An Old Man Can Regain His Youth*, pp. 26 ff.
32. Ibid.
33. Ibid.
34. Ibid., p. 30.
35. Ibid., pp. 22 ff.
36. *The Perfumed Garden*, pp. 158–59.

## CHAPTER 10

1. *The Glorious Koran*, p. 701. Other Koranic verses on the ambiguity about the sex of angels are:

19. And they make the angels, who are the slaves of the Beneficent, females.
    (Surah XLIII, "Ornaments of Gold," p. 647)

150. Or created We the angels females while they were present?
(Surah XXXVII, "Those Who Set the Ranks," p. 594)

2. The process of reproduction, the sex of angels, and the existence of goddesses in the sacred space of the pre-Islamic seventh-century Arabs are three closely linked themes that show the difficulties that Islam had to overcome as a monotheistic religion.
3. Nevertheless, it must be noted that the ambiguity about the sex of angels (because the divine being merely denies the suppositions of human beings without settling the question) is one of the rare instances of ambiguity in the Koran. Rationality is the essential and dominant quality of the Koran. Mystery or confusion are not phenomena that one often encounters in reading the Koran. When one does encounter an ambiguity, one remembers it, takes note of it, for the Koran, as a construction of the universe, has a crystalline limpidity. Relations and mechanisms, ensembles and components, have an almost mathematical coherence and a dazzling clarity. Islam's simplicity as doctrine has often been remarked upon. However, Islam is only simple for simpleminded people. As a construction of the universe, it is one of the most complex of mechanisms. But it is probably the clarity of the structure, the rationality that governs the mechanism and the relationships, that is perceived as simplicity. Compared to Christianity, for example, with its Trinity and mysteries (beginning with the one surrounding the life of its prophet), Islam is obviously simple, if simple means clear.
4. Ibn Khaldun, *Al-muqaddima* (Beirut: Al-Kitab al-Arabi, n.d.), p. 196.
5. See also the following Koranic verses:
   Surah XXXIV, "Saba," Verse 35, p. 567.
   Surah XXV, "The Criterion," Verse 74, p. 477.
   Surah LXIII, "The Hypocrites," Verse 9, p. 743.
   Surah IX, "Repentance," Verse 24, pp. 242–43.
   Surah LXVIII, "Victory," Verse 11, pp. 678–79.
   Surah LXIV, "Mutual Disillusion," Verse 15, p. 746.
6. See also the following Koranic verses, which refer to Adam's fall:
   Surah XV, "Al-Hijr," Verses 26–42, pp. 338–40.
   Surah XVII, "The Al-Isra," Verses 61–65, pp. 371–72.
   Surah XX, "Ta Ha," Verses 115–27, pp. 416–17.

# CHAPTER 11

1. The Moroccan Family Law will be used as an example for most of our illustrations here, because of all the Arab family laws it is the one where the contradictions between modernist aspirations and conservative allegiance to tradition are most striking, even to the point of caricature. For example, the Tunisian Family Law has chosen to underplay conservative elements and emphasize modern aspirations. Algeria is characterized by a notorious paralysis as far as family law is concerned, the so-called socialist Algerian state being still unable to produce a family law. The conflicts and tensions between modernists and traditionalists are such that the state is reduced to paralysis in this area, and with a striking regularity all projects to promulgate a new family law prove abortive.

2. *Al-Muduwana*, Dahir 1-57-343, Official Bulletin, 6 December 1957.
3. For descriptions of Paradise see also the following verses:
   Surah XLVII, "Muhammad," Verse 15, p. 673.
   Surah LXXXVIII, "The Overwhelming," Verses 8–16, p. 804.
   Surah LII, "The Mount," Verses 17–26, pp. 696–97.
   Surah XLIV, "Smoke," Verses 51–57, pp. 658–59.
   Surah LVI, "The Event," Verses 12–38, pp. 713–14.
   Surah LV, "The Beneficent," Verses 46–78, pp. 710–12.
   Surah XXXV, "The Angels," Verse 33, p. 575.
   Surah XXII, "The Pilgrimage," Verse 23, p. 435.
   Surah XVIII, "The Cave," Verses 30–31, p. 384.
   Surah XLIII, "Ornaments of Gold," Verses 70–72, p. 653.
4. See also Surah LII, "The Mount," Verse 20, p. 696.

## CHAPTER 12

1. Ibn al-Qalbi, *Kitab al-asnam* (Cairo: Matba'at Dar al-Kitab al-Misriya, 1924), p. 18. (Ibn al-Qalbi died in 204 A.H.)
   Regarding Al-Uzza, see also: Hartwig Derembourg, *Recueil des mémoires orientaux*, "Le culte de la déesse en Arabie du IVᵉ siècle de notre ére" (Paris, 1905).
2. Toufic Fahd, *Le Panthéon de l'Arabie centrale à la veille de l'hégire* (Paris: Geuthner, 1968), p. 164.
3. Ibid., p. 176.
4. Ibn al-Qalbi, *Kitab al-asnam*, pp. 13, 16.
5. See the commentary by William Montgomery Watt on the famous "satanic verses" in which the prophet acknowledged the female deities, verses that were later abrogated: William Montgomery Watt, *Muhammad at Mecca* (London: Oxford University Press, 1935), p. 104.
6. Ibn al-Qalbi, *Kitab al-asnam*, p. 19.
7. Ibid., p. 15.
8. Ibid., p. 17.
9. Ibid., p. 23.
10. Ibid., p. 25.
11. Ibid.
12. Ibid., p. 26.
13. Imam Bukhari, *Al-Sahih*. This passage is translated from the following source: O. Houdas, trans., *Al-Bukhari, traditions islamiques* (Paris: Imprimerie Nationale, 1908), vol. 3, p. 578.
14. The *takbir* is the ritual Islamic formula: "God is the greatest"; the *tahlil* is the ritual formula: "There is no god but God."
15. Imam Ghazzali, *Ihwa' 'ulum al-din*, pp. 49–50.
16. Ibid., p. 50.
17. Ibid.
18. Fatima Mernissi, *Beyond the Veil*, Chapter 2, "The Regulation of Female Sexuality in the Muslim Social Order," pp. 15–28.
19. Imam Bukhari, *Al-Sahih*, vol. 2, p. 217.

20. Ibid.
21. Jalal al-Din al-Suyuti, *Al-durar al-hisan wa na'im al-jinan*; Al-Imam Abd al-Rahman Ibn Ahmad al-Qadi, *Daqa'iq al-akhbar fi dhikr al-janna wal-nar*. (These two works are usually published together, one being presented as the annotation of the other.)
22. Ibn al-Qalbi, *Kitab al-asnam*, p. 46.
23. Imam Bukhari, *Al-Sahih*, p. 590 of the translation by O. Houdas.
24. Ibid., p. 600.
25. Imam Ghazzali, *Ihwa' 'ulum al-din*, p. 27.
26. The prohibition against homosexuality in Islam is expressed through the myth of Lot in, for example, the following surahs: Surah XXVI, "The Poets," Verses 165, 166; Surah XXVII, "The Ant," Verses 54, 55.
27. Understanding and deciphering "the Sign" is one of the key themes of the Koranic message. See for example: Surah II, "The Cow," Verses 248, 252, 259, 260; Surah III, "The Family of Imran," Verses 41, 49, 50, 58, 97, 103, 190; Surah IV, "Women," Verse 114. It also occurs in Surahs VI, VII, VIII, X, XI, XII, XIII, XIV, XV, XVI, XVII, XVIII, XIX, XX, XXI, XXII, XXIII, XXV, XXVI, XXVII, XXVIX, XXX, XXXI, XXXII, XXXIV, XXXVI, XXXVII, XXXIX, XL, XLI, XLII, XLIII, XLIV, XLV, XLVI, XLVII, XLVIII, LI, LIII, LIV, LVII, LXXIX.
28. See the list in Chapter 2 under the heading, "The discourse of chivalry: affective Islam or the world of sentiment," and Note 20 of that chapter. In the following pages, my analysis will focus on the two most coherent and elaborate of those texts: Imam Abd al-Rahman Ibn al-Jawzi, *Dhamm al-hawa* (the author lived in the thirteenth century of the Christian calendar); and Ibn Qayyim al-Jawzia, *Rawdat al-muhibbin wa nuzhat al-mushtaqin* (the author lived in the fourteenth century of the Christian calendar).
29. See Note 16, Chapter 2.
30. Ibn Qayyim al-Jawzia, *Rawdat al-muhibbin*, p. 19.
31. Ibid., p. 10.
32. Ibid., p. 9.
33. Ibid., p. 474.
34. Ibid., p. 475. (The verses to which he refers are the following: Surah VII, "The Heights," Verse 176; and Surah LXXIV, "The Cloaked One," Verses 50–51.)
35. Ibid., p. 474.
36. Imam Abd al-Rahman Ibn al-Jawzi, *Dhamm al-hawa*, p. 29.
37. Ibid., p. 24.
38. Ibid., p. 26.
39. Ibn Qayyim al-Jawzia, *Rawdat al-muhibbin*, p. 10.
40. Imam Abd al-Rahman Ibn al-Jawzi, *Dhamm al-hawa*, p. 39.
41. Ibn Qayyim al-Jawzia, *Rawdat al-muhibbin*, p. 477.
42. Imam Abd al-Rahman Ibn al-Jawzi, *Dhamm al-hawa*, p. 22. Regarding the importance of the notion of *muruwa*, see Ignaz Goldziher, *Muslim Studies* (Chicago: Aldine, 1967), Vol. 1, Chapter 1, "Introductory: Muruwwa and Din," pp. 11–44.
43. Imam Abd al-Rahman Ibn al-Jawzi, *Dhamm al-hawa*, p. 39.
44. Ibid., p. 24.
45. Ibn Qayyim al-Jawzia, *Rawdat al-muhibbin*, p. 3.
46. Ibid., p. 197.
47. Imam Abd al-Rahman Ibn al-Jawzi, *Dhamm al-hawa*, p. 29.

48. Ibid., p. 166.
49. Imam Bukhari, *Al-Sahih*, p. 554 of the translation by O. Houdas.
50. Imam Muslim, *Al-Sahih*, p. 29.
51. Ibid., p. 130.
52. Imam Ghazzali, *Ihwa' 'ulum al-din*, p. 57.
53. Ibid.
54. Ibid.
55. Ibid., p. 44.
56. This reduction of sexuality to genital friction reveals the fallacy of western male-staged "sexual liberation," which can be seen in solemn sex education courses in Swedish schools, as well as in Hugh Hefner's ridiculously pontifical publications and childish temples, the Playboy Clubs. A feminist liberation of sexuality, on the contrary, would reconstitute the wholeness of sexual beings: flesh, spirit, affect, esthetics, and so on.
57. Imam Muslim, *Al-Sahih*, p. 156.
58. Abu Dawud, *Al-Sunan* (Al-Matba'a al-Tazia: 1349 A.H.), Vol. 1, p. 355.
59. Imam Bukhari, *Al-Sahih*, p. 546 of the translation by O. Houdas.
60. Ibid.
61. Imam Ghazzali, *Ihwa' 'ulum al-din*, p. 30.
62. Ibid.
63. Ibid.
64. Imam Muslim, *Al-Sahih*, p. 156; Tarmidi, *Al-Sunan*, p. 416. Regarding the ban on sodomy, Tarmidi quotes the prophet as saying that "God has no regard for a man who has sodomized another hole, whether in man or woman" (p. 416).

    The wedding night is the subject of a whole genre of books for the young Muslim groom. They are small pamphlets, about twenty pages long, in which the religious authorities summarize the instructions on sexual matters that are found in the basic documents of the Sunna. These manuals for the young Muslim husband are available for a small price at the stands in front of mosques or from bookshops. For the two examples used in this study, see Note 21, Chapter 2.
65. Imam Bukhari, *Al-Sahih*, p. 590 of the translation by O. Houdas.
66. Tarmidi, *Al-Sunan*, p. 414.
67. Imam Ghazzali, *Ihwa' 'ulum al-din*, p. 32.

# Index